"Every manager should read this book!"

Dale Jeanes
Executive Vice President
BB&T Bank Corporation

"I have known Dr. Beitler for many years. He is the master of integrating complex concepts and practices into an easy-to-understand, easy-to-follow process. I highly recommend *Strategic Organizational Change*."

Dr. Nido R. Qubein
President, High Point University
Chairman, Great Harvest Bread Co.

"Change management is one of the most important tasks of managers today. Dr. Beitler's book provides helpful guidance for managers who are planning and implementing change. His book is easy to read, and is filled with useful information."

Dr. Thomas Peuntner
Manager, Industrial Relations
John Deere Corp.
Mannheim, Germany

"I have worked with Dr. Beitler for the past 15 years. His students, clients, and colleagues appreciate his ability to make the literature on organizational change and leadership practical and accessible. *Strategic Organizational Change* is Beitler at his best!"

Prof. Kevin B. Lowe
Burlington Industries Research Excellence Professor
Chairman, Department of Management
The Bryan School of Business & Economics
University of North Carolina at Greensboro

"Over the past decade, our working-professional students have praised *Strategic Organizational Change* for its step-by-step examples. I believe academics, practitioners, and students will appreciate the balance of theory and practice in this third edition."

Bradford R. Frazier, Ph.D.
Interim Director, MBA & MSL Programs
Pfeiffer University

"Much of the literature on organizational change and effectiveness focuses on theories with limited practical applicability or specific problems without an overarching framework and approach. Dr. Beitler offers specific solutions but always as part of his strategic approach to thinking and doing. I highly recommend his work."

Richard L. McElroy, Ph.D.
President
American Institute for Organizational Effectiveness

"This book has been such a valuable resource to my executive students that several commented that they plan to keep it as a working resource in their offices. Beitler's writing style is real and natural, not stuffy or overly academic. I reviewed several books on organizational change for my MBA class; Beitler's *Strategic Organizational Change* is my personal favorite."

Dr. Kevin Narramore
Los Angeles, CA

"*Strategic Organizational Change* is the only book that shows consultants and managers how to do organizational change. Believe me, after nearly 30 years of consulting, I have read them all!"

Tom Moore
Organizational Change Consultant

"*Strategic Organizational Change* is an extraordinary guide for leaders and managers who are responsible for leading change."

Phil Bowers, CEO
Professional Skills Development, Inc.

"I found *Strategic Organizational Change* to be an ideal text for my class. It covers all the essentials and gets to the heart of the issues quickly, without a lot of peripheral matter. Students appreciate this approach, and so do I."

Donald Hall, Ph.D.
Carleton University
Ottawa, Canada

"Mike's book contains valuable insights and systematic procedures we can use in our organization."

Steve Anderson
Vice President
Krispy Kreme Doughnut Corp.

"If you want to know more about how organizations work and how to be a more effective leader, this book is for you. Beitler's writing style is very comfortable, easy to process, yet academically thorough and sound. I use it regularly as a reference."

Dr. Paul Gerhardt, Jr.
"The Organizational Doctor"
Seattle, WA

"Being experienced in the chaos that poorly managed change can create within organizations, I fully appreciate the concise and insightful approach to managing change that Dr. Beitler takes in *Strategic Organizational Change*. Having completed countless change projects, I found myself nodding my head and laughing in places at the accurate, real-world examples Beitler uses. There were Aha moments too when he described incidents that helped me understand my own experiences more fully."

Richard A. Rorrer
Global Automotive Division
Tyco Electronics

Strategic Organizational Change

*A **Practitioner's** Guide*
for
Managers and Consultants

Third Edition

Michael A. Beitler, Ph.D.

PRACTITIONER PRESS INTERNATIONAL

Send inquires and orders for this book to:

P.O. Box 38353
Greensboro, NC 27438 USA

www.mikebeitler.com
or
www.ppi-bookstores.com

Library of Congress Control Number 2013939687
    1. Organizational Change — Management
    2. Organizational Effectiveness
    3. Consulting

ISBN 978-0-9726064-6-2

Printed in the United States of America

*I dedicate this book
to my parents,
Harry and Ruth Beitler*

Strategic Organizational Change

Acknowledgments

With each new edition, I must thank my new students, as well as my new and ongoing clients and colleagues for their helpful insights.

I owe a special thanks to Danyang Peng (my wife) and my children (Rebecca Grace, David Beitler, and Stephen Beitler) for their love, encouragement, and patience. Writing a book, and its subsequent editions, can be an obsession for an author; it has been for me.

While I can thank countless students, clients, and colleagues who have taught me so much over the years, I especially want to thank my following friends and colleagues:

Mr. John Allison	*Dr. Arlise McKinney*
Prof. Dr. Karl-Heinz Beissner	*Professor Bud Miles*
Dr. Bud Benscoter	*Dr. Lars Mitlacher*
Ms. Lenora Billings-Harris	*Professor Paul M. Muchinsky*
Professor E. Holly Buttner	*Prof. Dr. Walter Oechsler*
Dr. Markus Faller	*Dr. Thomas Peuntner*
Dr. Bradford Frazier	*Prof. Dr. Gerhard Raab*
Dr. Keith Grant	*Dr. Lars Reichmann*
Dr. Arun Gupta	*Dr. Ehap Sabri*
Professor Ronald Hunady	*Dr. Rick Shenkus*
Dr. Channelle James	*Ms. Gayle Smart*
Prof. Dr. Alfred Kieser	*Professor William Tullar*
Professor Huey B. Long	*Dr. Mary Pat Wylie*
Professor Kevin Lowe	*Professor Daniel Winkler*
Dr. Janis McFaul	*Dr. Preston Yarborough*

.

Preface

In the summer of 2001, I sat on the banks of the Rhein River writing the first edition of this book. I was serving as a Visiting Professor of Management at the University of Mannheim (Germany's number 1 ranked business school). This was a big change for a blue-collar American boy who grew up on the streets of Baltimore.

My life had gone through a lot of changes (most of them very positive) while the world appeared stable (and financially secure). Americans, and people around the world, were becoming wealthy; the stock market, real estate market, and our 401k statements told us everything was just fine.

Then on September 11, the world of stability and inevitable wealth seemed to evaporate before our eyes. This was followed by a stock market crash, real estate crash, and a near meltdown of our financial markets.

Since 2001, organizations have been faced with nonstop change, much of which has been unpleasant and anxiety-provoking. Everybody agrees that organizational change is inevitable. But organizational change does not have to be unpleasant and anxiety-provoking.

My goal in this book is to prepare you with the tools and mindset you'll need to lead or facilitate organizational change. It will make you a great asset to your organization or client, and give you a great sense of personal fulfillment.

Michael Beitler
Greensboro, NC, USA

Strategic Organizational Change

Brief Table of Contents

Detailed Table of Contents

CHAPTER 1

The Strategy-Driven Approach

In the first two editions of this book, I opened with a description of an encounter I had with a man at a local restaurant here in Greensboro, NC. It remains the best way I know of to tell you about my approach in this book:

In early 2001, I was working on the manuscript for this book in one of my favorite restaurants. While hunched over my papers in a nose-to-the-grindstone position, I sensed a shadow looming over me. I looked up at a well-dressed, business-type man who asked, "What are you working on so diligently?" I told him I was writing a book about systematically facilitating organizational change. His face went blank.

I hesitated, and said, "It's about managing change."

He instantly started laughing and sneered, "Why don't you write a book about managing the weather?"

I took a deep breath and asked, "Have there been any changes at your company lately?"

He sighed, sat down, and said, "Of course. Change is the only constant. Customers, suppliers, employees, stockholders, technology, demographics, governmental regulations, public opinion; they all change constantly. But you can't manage change; you can only react to it."

Most people in organizations have this same reactive approach to change, but I believe it is possible to be proactive and systematic. In this book, I will describe, step-by-step, how organizational change (OC) consultants can help managers to systematically lead organizational change.

Purpose of This Book

The purpose of this book is to provide consultants, managers, and students with a strategy-driven approach to the "real-life" practice of organizational change (OC). I am a practitioner writing to other practitioners: *consultants* (who facilitate organizational change efforts), *managers* (who lead organizational change efforts), and *students* (who are the future facilitators and leaders of organizational change efforts).

Since effective practice is built upon a solid theoretical foundation, the study of organizational change practice should be preceded by the successful completion of at least the following two college-level courses: Principles of Management and Organizational Behavior (or Organizational Psychology). Some additional courses that will help build a strong theoretical foundation for effective practice include Strategic Management, Organizational Design & Theory, Leadership Assessment & Development, and Group Dynamics.

Every effective OC practitioner I have known has a strong theoretical foundation to build his or her practice upon. We will briefly review the most important theoretical foundations in Chapter 2.

Consultant/Facilitator Viewpoint

While it is possible to take two different approaches to studying OC, consultant/facilitator versus manager/leader, I have decided to consistently use the consultant/facilitator viewpoint. The consultant/facilitator has the responsibility of guiding the organizational members (including managers) through the change process from data gathering and diagnosis to implementation and evaluation.

Throughout this book, I will emphasize the important role of the OC consultant as a "process" facilitator. The consultant serves as facilitator and coach, while management makes the final "content" decisions. This important distinction between process and content will be discussed at length in Chapter 3. Building a collaborative relationship between consultant and management is Chapter 3's focus.

Chapter 4 is devoted to leading change. Leading change is the responsibility of the organization's senior management. "Facilitating" change efforts and coaching management on the change process are the proper roles for the OC consultant. How to coach (and educate) management members on the change process is the focus of Chapter 4.

Step-by-Step Process

The work of the OC consultant follows the six-step Action Research Model. We will discuss the Action Research Model at length in Chapter 2.

The first step of the Action Research Model, data gathering, is discussed, in a step-by-step manner, in Chapter 5. Both methods and sources of data gathering will be discussed in a practitioner checklist manner.

The second, third, and fourth steps in the Action Research Model are feedback to the client, diagnosis with the client, and action planning with the client. These steps are covered in Chapter 6.

The fifth step involves the interventions or "tools" that are used to implement change. Fortunately, there are many tools available to the OC consultant. I have divided the OC interventions (tools) into four types. The four types of interventions (strategic, structural, cultural, and human processes) are covered in Part II of the book (Chapters 7-12).

The final step in the Action Research Model is evaluation. In Chapter 13, I provide guidelines on how to evaluate both the OC intervention and the OC consultant.

The last chapter is devoted to emerging issues in OC practice. The two most important issues facing practitioners today are globalization and new technology. Chapter 14 is the result of my discussions with numerous OC consultants and managers.

Three Roots of OC Practice

The practice of OC has been disjointed, unsystematic, and, to a large extent, ineffective. Three "camps" of consultants have developed their practices without the benefit of each other's knowledge or practice tools.

The field of OC has three clearly distinct roots: Management Advisory Services (MAS), Organizational Learning (OL), and Organization Development (OD). These three camps have not worked well together because the practitioners in each subfield have had very different backgrounds and orientations.

Management Advisory Services (MAS) has been practiced by large management consulting firms for many years. These management consultants have been assisting clients in developing strategic plans and in reorganizing corporate structures. These strategic and structural changes have had a distinctively business-like bottomline orientation.

Organizational Learning (OL) practitioners specialize in developing what has become known as learning organizations. Like MAS, OL takes a big picture approach to change. OL practitioners hope to create and maintain an atmosphere of continuous acquisition and dissemination of knowledge throughout the organization. Virtually all businesses today, especially high-performance companies, are continuously learning (and changing) to stay competitive.

The literature on organizational learning speaks of individuals learning new KSAs (knowledge, skills, and attitudes) for the benefit of the organization. For the organization to benefit, the new learning must be "captured" and made available to organizational members (Beitler, 2000, 2010).

Finally, **Organization Development (OD)** practitioners focus on diagnosing and changing human interactions between individuals and within groups (French & Bell, 1999). We should recognize the behavioral science roots of OD. OD practitioners have learned (and continue to learn) much from the behavioral science disciplines of psychology, sociology, and anthropology.

Organization Development (OD) deals with the business organization's human process issues (opportunities as well as problems). These issues include team building, conflict management, decision making, and communication, among others.

All three of these roots (MAS, OL, and OD) have something to offer OC consultants. Unfortunately, the three roots of current OC practice have not been brought together into a systematic practice model.

PRACTICE LOG 1.1 — My History with Change Efforts
I started my career with an international management consulting firm. As a CPA, I was initially assigned to auditing and accounting engagements. While I clearly saw the importance of this work, I did not find it to be very fulfilling. I didn't feel that I was making an impact on the organization's future effectiveness.

Eventually, I had the opportunity to work in the firm's MAS (management advisory services) practice with a variety of clients of different sizes in different industries. I found this "big picture" work to be much more interesting. Developing strategic plans and reorganizing the structures of entire organizations was very exciting for a young consultant.

Eventually, however, I began to question the effectiveness of these grandiose plans and restructurings. Was anything really changing? Clearly, there was little change in the financial statements. In many cases, the financial statements actually looked worse. When I questioned my superiors, I got responses equivalent to "you're too young to understand, these things take time." But as I watched these companies quarter after quarter (and year after year) I didn't see any dramatic changes. In fact, the only changes I saw in many client organizations were increases in employee complaints about management, and longings for the "good ole days." Was there a problem with MAS's approach to change?

After several years of practicing the MAS approach to change at the management consulting firm, I spent ten years as a senior vice president in banking. As an "insider," I found implementing change to be equally frustrating.

Then after my banking career, I became involved in change consulting from the OL and OD approaches. It soon seemed obvious — both of these approaches also offered only pieces of a larger puzzle.

Finally, after many years of frustration as both consultant/facilitator and manager/leader of change efforts, I developed a systematic strategy-driven approach to organizational change. I want to share that approach with you in this book.

The Strategy-Driven Approach

The strategy-driven approach to organizational change assumes that every organization is more effective when "all the horses are pulling in the same direction." Team building, conflict resolution, or restructuring interventions are doomed to failure until all the organizational members are aware of the organization's mission and its strategy to fulfill that mission.

The first step for the OC consultant is to be sure the organization has a well-crafted strategic plan that clearly communicates how senior management intends to fulfill the organization's mission. Frequently, the organization has a vague mission and/or an unrealistic strategic plan. In these cases, the OC consultant should recommend a strategic planning session with the senior management team. How to facilitate the strategic planning process is the focus of Chapter 7.

Once assured the organization has a well-crafted, well-communicated strategic plan, the OC consultant must determine if the current organizational structure, culture, and human processes will support the strategy. Invariably, attempts to implement even the best-crafted strategy will fail if the organization's structure, culture, and human processes are not supportive.

I developed the following model to show the relationship between these four aspects (a model that I modify a bit later):

Strategy	
Structure	**Processes**
Culture	

FIGURE 1.1

If a well-crafted, well-communicated organizational strategic plan is in place, it is possible to make changes in the other three areas that result in dramatic improvement in organizational effectiveness.

We will discuss structural changes in Chapter 8. It is possible to make structural changes at three levels in the organization: the entire organization level, the subsystem level (department, group, team), and the individual job or role level.

Chapter 9 will be devoted to changing organizational culture. I have put culture on the bottom of my model because all organizational activities are rooted in the organization's culture. Organizational culture is a powerful and pervasive force in every organization. The different interventions, both direct and indirect, for changing organizational culture will be covered in a step-by-step manner.

Chapters 10 through 12 cover process interventions. Two of my German colleagues from the University of Mannheim, Markus Faller and Lars Mitlacher, have stressed the importance of making a clear distinction between human process interventions and technical (operational) interventions. Their insights led to the following modification to my original model:

Strategy		
Structure	**Human Processes**	**Technical Processes**
Culture		

FIGURE 1.2

Human process interventions include making the following types of changes:

Team Building
Conflict Management
Decision Making/Problem Solving
Communication
Management Development
Organizational Learning

Technical (operational) interventions include the following types of changes:

Production
Engineering
Finance
Logistics
Technology
Technical interventions, while very important to organizational effectiveness, are beyond the scope of this book. Technical interventions require content expertise.

Strategy		
Structure	Human Processes	~~Technical Processes~~
Culture		

FIGURE 1.3

It is essential to understand that OC consultants are process facilitators, not content experts. Process consultants (like me) can help facilitate changes in strategy, structure, culture, or human processes, without claiming any content expertise about a specific industry or technical process. This important distinction will be discussed further in Chapter 3.

In this book, we will use the following model to discuss the four different types of organizational change interventions:

Strategy	
Structure	Human Processes
Culture	

FIGURE 1.4: Targets for Change

There are an extremely large number of human process interventions available for OC consultants and their clients. We cannot possibly cover all of them in this book. In Chapter 10 we will discuss team building and conflict management interventions. In Chapter 11 we will cover management development interventions. And in Chapter 12 we will detail organizational learning interventions.

The proper alignment of these four organizational aspects (strategy, structure, culture, and human processes) cannot be over emphasized. My model of these four targets for change, and the importance of aligning these four organizational aspects, will be revisited throughout this book.

Growing Need for OC Consultants

As the world we live in changes at an increasingly rapid rate (I'll have more to say about this in Chapter 14), the need for OC consultants to facilitate organizational change will continue to grow. Using the systematic approach I offer in this book, I think you will find this work to be exciting and immensely rewarding.

Let's get started by looking at the foundational concepts of successful OC practice in Chapter 2. (I believe even experienced practitioners should find this to be a helpful review.)

REFERENCES

Beitler, M.A. (2000). Contract learning in organizational learning and management development. In H.B. Long & Associates (Eds.), *Practice and theory in self-directed learning*. Schaumberg, IL: Motorola University Press.

Beitler, M.A. (2010). *Strategic organizational learning (2nd ed.)*. Greensboro, NC: Practitioner Press International.

French, W.L. & Bell, C.H., Jr. (1999). *Organization development: Behavioral science interventions for organization improvement* (6th ed.). Upper Saddle River, NJ: Prentice-Hall.

CHAPTER 2

Foundations of OC Practice: A Brief Review

The study of OC should be focused on practice. Senior managers at today's organizations will not pay for theory alone. Fortunately, many highly effective "tools" (interventions) have been developed for our use in practice. But these do not excuse OC consultants from knowing the concepts underlying effective OC practice. OC has a substantial research-based conceptual foundation that supports effective OC practice. OC consultants need to know these concepts.

Let me begin by presenting my model of how OC concepts support practice theory, which, in turn, leads to effective practice. Then I will discuss the relevance of each concept to practice theory and to practice itself.

FIGURE 2.1 Foundations of OC Practice

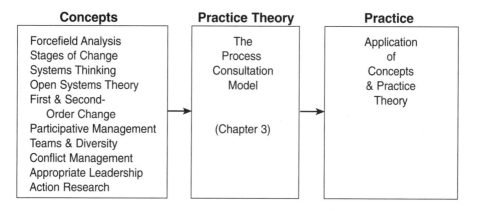

The ten concepts in the model are interrelated. The value of Schein's Process Consultation Practice Model (discussed in Chapter 3) is in its integration of these foundational concepts into a coherent Practice Model.

Let's take a look at each of these ten foundational concepts.

1. Forcefield Analysis

Kurt Lewin, the consummate applied social scientist, is responsible for giving us three of the ten concepts that support effective OC practice: Forcefield Analysis, The Three-Stage Model of Change, and the Action Research Model.

Lewin's first concept, and practice tool, is called Forcefield Analysis. Lewin believed every organizational situation, no matter how dysfunctional, benefits someone. I have found this concept and tool to be very effective in OC practice.

Lewin believed the status quo is a result of driving forces and resisting forces. See the illustration below.

FIGURE 2.2 Lewin's Forcefield Analysis

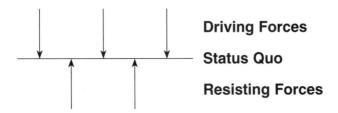

Driving forces are pushing or "driving" for change. Resisting forces exist because some parties benefit from the current situation, or status quo. Thus, the status quo is the result of the strengths of the two opposing forces.

In practice, Lewin recommended working to reduce the resisting forces, instead of increasing the driving forces. He believed simply increasing the driving forces would result in an escalation in the resisting forces against the change. The parties resisting change (supporting the status quo) are usually highly motivated.

PRACTICE LOG 2.1 — "Gandhi?"

The best example of Lewin's idea of reducing the resisting forces, instead of increasing the driving forces, comes from one of my students.

During one of my evening classes, I had just finished explaining Lewin's Forcefield Analysis (complete with an illustration on the blackboard showing arrows pushing against each other). As I paused to think of a corporate example of reducing the resisting forces instead of increasing the driving forces, one excited student shouted out: "That's what Gandhi did!"

Frankly, I was completely baffled by his confident statement. My other students, equally surprised by his comment, turned to look at him. Then they looked at my blank face.

"Excuse me," I muttered.

"Sure," he continued, "Gandhi could have given an inspiring speech to rally the Indian forces against the British. But increasing the driving forces for change would have lead to a crushing defeat. The British leaders would have resisted by bringing in highly trained soldiers from all over their empire."

My student's excellent example of using Forcefield Analysis to diagnose a situation provides instructive guidance for all of us. Clearly, the first step for the OC practitioner, when using Forcefield Analysis, is to determine who or what the driving and resisting forces are.

2. Stages of Change (The Three-Step Model)

Another concept closely associated with Forcefield Analysis is what Lewin called the Three-Step Model of Change. He believed change required three steps: unfreezing the current situation, moving, and then refreezing the new situation (a new status quo). At first glance, this may appear to be obvious and simplistic. But the steps are very important.

The OC consultant must first help the organization to see the dysfunctionality (ineffectiveness) of the current situation. Remember, we are dealing with some organizational members who benefit from the current status quo.

To move the organization or the unit (to change behavior) requires a planned intervention. This will be a time of insecurity and fear for many organizational members. Fortunately, there are many structured interventions available to OC consultants. (We will cover interventions in Part II of this book.)

In step three, Lewin said we must "refreeze" the situation. In practice, I have found this step to be essential. In order to get the change to hold, there must be a supportive environment for the change. This means management must commit resources and reward desired behaviors; otherwise, the organizational members will slip back into their old, comfortable ways of doing things.

Anthony Buono (2000) has correctly added, "There is a significant difference between dealing with the type of episodic, discontinuous change that Lewin referred to in 1947, when he created this model (dealing, in essence, with organizational inertia), and the type of ongoing, overlapping, continuous change that is happening today." I will expound on Professor Buono's comment in the chapter on Leading Change.

3. Systems Thinking

Systems thinking is important for OC practitioners (and managers) because rarely is there an "evil" person in the organization bent on bringing pain and destruction. Bad behavior, or ineffective behavior, is often unwittingly rewarded by management. Protecting turf, not communicating with peers, not contributing to the team, high absenteeism, and resisting change happen for a reason.

In many organizations (especially in American organizations), the management team goes "headhunting" immediately after an error occurs or a problem arises. "Heads will roll!" they declare. The assumption is that there is a bad person causing the problem; if they get rid of the person, they get rid of the problem.

More often than not, the person is not "the problem." The problem is typically embedded in the system. If we don't change the system, we will soon face the same problem again.

PRACTICE LOG 2.2 — Lessons from Other Professionals
Systems theory was not originally developed by OC practitioners. Systems theory has roots in the early theories of physical scientists.

They correctly understood that physical phenomena don't operate in a closed vacuum; physical phenomena continuously interact with other phenomena in any given system.

Fortunately, the wisdom of systems theory did not start and end with the physical scientists. Social scientists, including sociologists and psychologists, have also adopted a systems approach.

Systems thinking has been a highly effective tool of counselors with at-risk youths. "At-risk youths" is a nice way of talking about the types of teenagers who frighten us (at risk for drug use, teenage pregnancy, or a life of crime). Many frustrated counselors were devoting many hours to these youths. Typically, after these youths faced up to their problems, and committed to changing their behavior, they were sent home. But with alarming predictability, these at-risk youths reverted to their old behaviors. Why? Were they insincere about change?

Counselors eventually realized that sending these youths back to the same abusive fathers, alcoholic mothers, and drug-abusing friends was inviting failure. The youths needed support for their new behavior; that meant changing the system. Counselors began counseling the entire family. Changing the system (the family) has been much more effective.

Organizational change consultants and managers must take the same systemic approach. Peter Senge (1990) is often quoted for his work on organizational learning. Personally, I believe Senge's larger contribution is in the application of systems thinking to business organizations. Systemic change involves a lot of work, but the change is powerful and lasting.

4. Open Systems

Open systems theory takes systems thinking one step further. Systems Theory changes our diagnostic focus from the individual to the system. Open Systems Theory helps us recognize the fact that the system itself is embedded in another, larger system. This larger system, its environment, exerts substantial influence on the organization.

As OC practitioners we may see system-wide problems that exist within the walls of the organization, but we must remain aware of the environment in which the organization operates. A business organization's environment includes its customers, suppliers, competitors, government regulators, and so on.

5. *First & Second-Order Change*

Organizational change practices are gaining wider acceptance among corporate senior managers because these leaders recognize the crucial importance of responding quickly to change. Organizations must respond to two types of change: second-order change and first-order change.

Second-order change is discussed more in management literature because it is dramatic, radical, and revolutionary. The very survival of the organization may depend on these changes. Examples of second-order change include interventions to create and implement a new corporate mission or to completely restructure the organization's hierarchy. Second-order changes occur rather infrequently, but they get the attention of many interested parties (investment analysts, customers, employees, suppliers, competitors).

First-order change, while equally important, gets less attention. It is less dramatic, incremental, and evolutionary in nature. But these "developmental" changes should be occurring on a continual basis. First-order changes should continue after the dramatic, large-scale, second-order changes have been successfully implemented (long after the investment analysts and the media disappear). Examples of first-order changes include interventions to reduce intergroup conflict or to build cross-functional teams.

Organizational change requires organizational flexibility. Change and flexibility are more important to organizational success than ever before. The Industrial Age was dominated by assembly lines and "one-best-way" production processes. This worked well in organizations where the goal was to produce as many unchanging "widgets" as possible. When international competition was virtually non-existent, and consumers bought anything that was available, change was infrequent and slow. But today, inflexible production processes or rigid organizational hierarchies spell disaster in industries where innovative, consumer-oriented strategies are required.

6. Participative Management

I recently read an article in which the author said, "Senior managers are becoming more accepting of participative management and employee involvement because they (senior managers) are becoming more humanistic." Nonsense!

Anybody who works with senior managers as a management consultant quickly realizes that most managers enjoy the power vested in their positions. Many of these managers are not interested in sharing their power and decision-making authority. OC consultants who argue for participative management and employee involvement for humanistic reasons will surely meet resistance.

Nido Qubein, in his audiotapes on marketing professional services, said, "don't appeal to somebody's better nature; he or she may not have one." OC consultants must help managers see how they (the managers) will benefit from participative management and employee involvement.

Participation and involvement of employees at every level of the organization has become critical for organizations to develop and maintain a competitive advantage. The continuously changing demands for new and improved products and services require the utilization of the mental skills and emotional commitment of each organizational member. It has become simply impossible for single managers to "micro-manage" the complex operations they are responsible for. Gone are the days when companies hired and managed "hands."

Employee empowerment (shared responsibility and authority) is now a critical skill for management. Management must facilitate the work processes and development of its employees. The change in the role of managers from controllers to facilitators has been difficult for many managers. This change has created coaching opportunities for OC consultants.

PRACTICE LOG 2.3 — $2,000 Per Day for a Short Walk

One of my earliest, and most valuable, lessons in the importance of participative management and employee involvement came from Rick. Rick is my mentor in consulting.

Rick told me about sitting in on a management meeting of one of his manufacturing clients. The conversation of the management members turned to production problems. They could not figure out why their production output was dramatically below their competitors'. Production numbers were far below the engineering predictions for new equipment. They explained to Rick how they had designed and redesigned the production process, with no success.

After many years of consulting, Rick has a "nose" for this kind of problem. Rick said, "Give me a week; I'll tell you how to fix the problem." Since the management members saw Rick as a consultant for "people problems," they appeared a bit surprised and amused. But the frustrated and somewhat desperate CEO said, "OK, give me a report by next Friday." I should point out that Rick charges $300 per hour or $2,000 per day, plus expenses.

For the next four-and-a-half days, Rick entered the client's breakroom at 8 am, drank a cup of coffee, then walked down the hallway to the production facility. He talked to the machine operators individually and in groups. He talked to supervisors. He even learned how to run the new machines (or at least got familiar with the new machines). On Friday afternoon he put his report on the CEO's desk.

The following week, Rick got a phone call from the CEO who sang Rick's praises as a brilliant consultant. What did Rick's report say? Rick's report simply told the managers what the employees (the people doing the job) thought about how to improve the job.

When he told me this story, I stopped him and exclaimed, "Wait a minute! You charged the company $10,000 to walk down the hallway and get the answers from its own employees? The managers could have done that themselves."

"I suggested that," Rick replied, "the managers ignored that as a possibility."

Was Rick right to collect the $10,000? He ultimately saved the company hundreds of thousands of dollars with the new processing procedures. Arrogance cost that company $10,000!

Employee involvement would have saved it $10,000.

7. *Teams & Diversity*

As the last section indicates, an organization needs the full participation and involvement of its members. Teams become meaningless collections of individuals without active participation and involvement.

Teams have become a popular way to structure organizational members and work processes, but teams are not always appropriate. (We will discuss the appropriate uses of teams in a later chapter.)

Much of the excitement about teams was in reaction to the incredible success of Japanese manufacturers. Many American organizations tried to copy the Japanese example, with little thought about the impact of culture. The success of teams in the U.S. has been limited. I will have more to say about the impact of national culture on OC efforts later in this book.

There is something about the nature of teams that all OC consultants and managers should be aware of. The major advantage and the major disadvantage are two sides of the same coin. The major advantage of teams is diversity. The major disadvantage of teams is diversity. Let me explain.

Organizations benefit when diverse organizational members bring different viewpoints to the table. Cross-functional teams, made up of members from various organizational functions (i.e. finance, production, marketing, HR), can be highly creative and innovative. No one individual could possibly match a cross-functional team's experience, expertise, and diverse viewpoints.

But diversity is also the disadvantage of teams. When you bring together diverse viewpoints, conflict is inevitable. So, to benefit from the advantages of teams, organizations must learn to manage the inevitable conflict.

8. Conflict Management

As stated above, conflict management is extremely important to the effective operation of the organization. Notice that we are talking about conflict management, not conflict elimination. Attempts to eliminate conflict result in the reluctance of members to express diverse or differing opinions. Eliminating conflict would eliminate one of the major benefits of teams — diverse or differing opinions. OC consultants play important roles in teaching and facilitating effective conflict management.

Later in this book, we will discuss the interventions OC consultants can use to help organizations manage conflict.

9. Appropriate Leadership

There is a huge amount of literature on leadership. Some of it is quite good and worth reading (Goldman, 2000; Ulrich, 1999). Some of it is just silly. OC practitioners and managers should read the literature that is well-researched and based on sound, established principles. They should avoid the management *fad du jour*.

One sound, established principle of effective leadership is the leadership style should be appropriate for the situation. OC practitioners should not enter new organizations looking for (or advocating) their favorite management/leadership style. I have worked with many abrasive managers who were highly respected and extraordinarily successful. The fact that I found them offensive has nothing to do with improving organizational effectiveness. An OC consultant should help clients promote appropriate management styles that maximize productivity and worker satisfaction in the clients' particular organization.

It is generally agreed that there are two extremes in management/leadership styles, as depicted below:

FIGURE 2.3 — The Continuum of Management Styles

Manager-Directed	Employee-Directed
(autocratic)	(laissez-faire)

The autocratic extreme is characterized by the boss barking out orders and the employees quickly obeying without questioning. The laissez-faire (hands-off) extreme is characterized by the boss who lets the employees "do their thing" without interrupting or commenting. Obviously these are the extremes, and neither one is typically appropriate in practice.

In business schools, first and foremost, we emphasize that there is no such thing as one best management/leadership style. There are countless effective management styles based on varying degrees of manager-direction and employee-participation. The style chosen should be appropriate for the situation.

Determining the appropriate management style is actually quite complicated. So, I offer my students a checklist for making the determination. Three elements must be considered: (1) the manager's characteristics, (2) the employees' characteristics, and (3) the task's characteristics. The resulting checklist looks like the following:

FIGURE 2.4 — The Management Style Checklist

	Manager- Directed	Employee- Directed
1. The manager's characteristics		
knowledge	high	low
experience	high	low
2. The employees' characteristics		
knowledge	low	high
experience	low	high
maturity level	low	high
motivation level	low	high
ability to set goals	low	high
3. The task's characteristics		
clarity of the goal	low	high
time availability	low	high
resource availability	low	high

Circling items on the left side of the **Management Style Checklist** indicates a need to move to the left (manager-directed) side of the **Continuum of Management Styles.** Circling items on the right side of the Checklist indicates a need to move to the right (employee-directed) side of the Continuum.

Can a manager with low knowledge and low experience still be an effective leader? Yes. He or she can still serve the needs of employees with high knowledge and experience, in various tasks, if he/she is willing to serve in the role of facilitator (instead of in the role of subject matter expert).

Obviously, my Checklist oversimplifies reality. In practice, it may be necessary to consider ten continua (one for each item) to properly reflect the complexity of the particular situation. It is important not to think of manager-directed or employee-directed in terms of which one is better. There is not an ideal management/leadership style for every task and situation; we must think in terms of the *appropriate style*.

PRACTICE LOG 2.4 "One Size Fits All?"
At the age of 31, I was promoted to Senior Vice President/Chief Financial Officer of the bank I worked for. I was delighted; then terrified. I was suddenly the #3 guy in a well-established, highly profitable organization that was older than I was.

I began to talk, walk, and dress like the other senior executives. Copying their style made sense to me. Sure, it worked for them. You can probably see several mistakes in my reasoning. They were older, more knowledgeable, more experienced, and wiser than I.

The autocratic style I adopted (copied) worked quite well with some employees, in some situations. But more often than not, I was met with tremendous resistance. And because I was operating outside of my comfort zone all day, I could be seen dragging myself to my car late every evening.

I wish I had owned a copy of the Management Style Checklist then. I learned the hard way about analyzing the manager's characteristics (my characteristics), the employees' characteristics, and the task characteristics. One management style does not fit all situations.

Let me add one more consideration that will complicate this a little further. A limitation of my Checklist is that it only provides a "snapshot" at a point in time (like the company's balance sheet). Hopefully, employees will become more knowledgeable, experienced, and mature; therefore, a move toward the right side of the Continuum is natural over time.

10. Action Research

The last concept I want to share is more than a concept. Action Research is a basic practice model. A practice model provides the practice theories and guidelines we need to effectively practice our profession.

Action Research is another contribution of Kurt Lewin. (Lewin also gave us the first two concepts in this chapter: Forcefield Analysis and the Three-Stage Model of Change.)

It is important to keep in mind the role of the OC consultant. The OC consultant is an expert in *process*, not *content*.

Organizational change consultants specialize in diagnosing and improving the people processes that support the successful implementation of the organization's strategic plan. Generally speaking, OC consultants do not have expertise in the *content* areas of a particular business: manufacturing processes, marketing, finance, accounting, or information technology (IT). OC consultants have an ethical responsibility to refer their clients to content experts for questions in these areas.

Lewin's model indicates the critical importance of establishing and maintaining a collaborative partnership with the client to jointly diagnose and intervene in organizational problem areas. The Action Research Model provides the general framework for OC practice; Schein's Process Consultation Model provides detailed practice guidelines. (We will devote Chapter 3 to Schein's practice model.)

Let's briefly look at the steps in Lewin's Action Research Model. Be sure to "dog-ear" this page! We will be referring back to the Action Research Model throughout this book.

FIGURE 2.5 — Action Research Steps

1. Data Gathering — From Client Members
2. Data Feedback — To Client Members
3. Diagnosis — With Client Members
4. Action Planning — With Client Members
5. Action Taking/Interventions — With Client Members
6. Evaluating — With Client Members

Gathering data from the client will be covered in Chapter 5. Data feedback, diagnosis, and action planning with the client will be the topics of Chapter 6.

Action taking and interventions will be addressed in detail in Chapters 7 through 12. Chapter 13 will cover the process of evaluating OC efforts.

Let's move on to Chapter 3 in which we examine Schein's Process Consultation Model, a model for successful OC practice.

References

Buono, A. (2000). Personal correspondence.

Goldman, D. (2000). Leadership that gets results. *Harvard Business Review*, March-April.

Senge, P. M. (1990). *The fifth discipline: The art and practice of the learning organization.* New York: Doubleday.

Ulrich, D. (1999). *Results-based leadership.* Boston: Harvard Business School Press.

CHAPTER 3

Process Consulting: A Practice Model

I have two heroes in the field of OC: Kurt Lewin and Edgar Schein. I introduced Lewin's Action Research Model in Chapter 2. Action Research provides a model for consultants to effectively apply social science principles to help their clients.

Edgar Schein has built upon Lewin's work and developed a practice model for OC consultants (and for anybody who serves as a helper). Schein (1999) calls his practice model "Process Consultation" (PC). PC is not mere theory, but a map for helpers to navigate the tricky waters of human interactions.

Three Consulting Approaches

Schein (1999) believes there are basically three approaches to helping: the expert model, the doctor-patient model, and the process consultation (PC) model.

In the expert model, the client diagnoses the problem and then purchases the expertise of a consultant. This is appropriate in some situations. If a company determines it needs an intranet system to enhance its in-house communications, it should purchase the expertise of an IT consultant (based on its own diagnosis).

But the appropriate use of the expert model is based on several assumptions:

1. The **client** can properly diagnose the problem.
2. The client can properly communicate the relevant facts to the consultant.
3. The client understands the effect on the organization of turning the problem over to the consultant.
4. The client understands the consequences of implementing the

consultant's recommended changes.

The doctor-patient (or physician) model also has appropriate and inappropriate applications. In this model, the patient/client simply describes symptoms. Then the physician/consultant diagnoses the problem and decides on a solution. This model may be appropriate (in some cases required) when the patient/client has little or no knowledge to contribute to the physician/consultant's decision.

But the appropriate use of the physician model is also based on certain assumptions:

1. The **consultant** can properly diagnose the problem.
2. The client can properly communicate the relevant facts to the consultant.
3. The client understands the effect on the organization of turning the problem over to the consultant.
4. The client understands the consequences of implementing the consultant's recommended changes.

While the expert and doctor-patient models are widely used by consultants, both models are inappropriate for OC practitioners. OC consultants are not *content* experts, but *process* consultants.

The third model, developed and advocated by Schein, is Process Consultation (PC). In the PC model, the consultant immediately involves the client as a partner. The consultant and client collaboratively diagnose the problem, design and implement interventions, and evaluate the success of the interventions.

Schein (1999) lists several guidelines for consultant success with the PC model:

1. The consultant must communicate that the client "owns" the problem.
2. The consultant and client must work together as equal partners throughout the OC process.
3. The client knows what will and will not work in its culture, so client participation and "buy-in" are essential.

4. The consultant must diligently check out the "presenting problem," plus any preconceptions and expectations.

The PC model offers several advantages for the OC consultant:

1. The OC consultant does **not** have to be a content (marketing, production, logistics, finance, etc.) expert to be helpful.

2. The OC consultant does **not** have to decide what the client must do. The OC consultant facilitates the client's decision-making-process.

3. The client's valuable input is available throughout the OC process.

EXERCISE 3.1 — How Do You Help?

1. Think back over the last few days and identify one instance of someone's asking for your help or advice.

2. Reconstruct the conversation in your own mind.
   What did the other person want?
   How did you respond?
   What role did you take? (expert, "physician," process consultant)
   Could you have responded differently?

3. Pair up with a partner and tell your stories. Listen to your partner's reaction to what he or she observed in your behavior.

4. Analyze his or her response to your story from the point of view of what role they thought you took. How did you react to his or her response?

5. Reverse roles. Listen to your partner's story. Respond to your partner's story. What reactions did you elicit from your partner?

6. Reflect on the roles that you seem to take naturally and spontaneously when someone seeks your help. Are there other roles that you should learn to take?

Source: Schein, E.H. (1999). *Processing consultation revisited: Building the helping relationship*. Reading, MA: Addison-Wesley OD Series. (p.29).

The Psychodynamics of Helping

In any helping relationship, there are several possible reactions by the helper (consultant) and the helped (client). Unfortunately, many of these reactions are highly destructive to the effectiveness of the relationship.

The possible negative reactions of the client include resentment and defensiveness, or relief and dependency. Resentment and defensiveness lead the client to look for opportunities to make the consultant look bad. The client may challenge and resist all of the consultant's input.

The client may also react with relief and dependency. Relief is usually expressed as, "I'm so glad you're here." Then the client drops a stack of file folders in the consultant's lap and runs down the hallway. Dependency is expressed by a client helplessly saying, "I don't have any ideas, you are the expert."

Schein (1999) warns consultants about the "Power Vacuum." The power vacuum is how Schein illustrates the possibility of the consultant getting "sucked in" to taking responsibility for the client's problem.

These destructive client reactions are often exacerbated by the consultant's reactions. Client defensiveness is often met with consultant defensiveness and additional pressure to agree with the "expert." I once heard a consultant condescendingly say, "I don't think you understood my suggestion; let me explain it in a simpler way that you can understand."

Consultants are often guilty of accepting and encouraging client dependency. Comments like, "Don't you worry about it, I'll take care of everything," foster client dependency. Frankly, some consultants enjoy the power and authority that is ascribed to the expert.

One more issue to keep in mind here: transference and counter-transference (please excuse the Freudian terminology). Transference involves the client's perceiving the consultant as a parent, school teacher, or some past negative authority figure. Counter-transference involves the consultant's perceiving the client as a past negative client.

It is important that the consultant remain aware of the current psychodynamics occurring between him/herself and the client. It is essential that a collaborative and cooperative relationship be established and maintained.

Write Down "All the Things You Don't Know"

Perhaps the strangest sounding, but most helpful, of Schein's advice is to write down "all the things you don't know" (1999, p.41). That's right — don't know! As consultants or helpers we are accustomed to writing down everything we do know. But according to Schein, this habit can get the consultant into trouble. The consultant writes down several things he or she knows, and then makes a confident but premature recommendation.

This idea of Schein's has saved me on many occasions. As a consultant, I frequently feel time pressure from the client. They are paying by the hour (or day) so they are understandably concerned about time and, ultimately, fees.

Time pressure on the client leads to time pressure on the OC consultant. The consultant is subtly (and often not so subtly) pressured for quick solutions to problems. It is not uncommon for a client to offer a few sketchy details, and then ask expectantly, "What do you think?" The OC consultant now runs the risk of making a big mistake: a premature, ill-prepared recommendation.

By writing down all the things I don't know, I can slow down the process. Both parties benefit from my "don't know list":

1. I, the consultant, can clearly see that I don't have enough information to make a recommendation.

2. The client clearly sees that the consultant has legitimate questions about the situation. Frequently, the client realizes that he or she has not even considered these questions.

By writing down all the things we don't know, we take the focus off time and place it on building a collaborative working relationship.

EXERCISE 3.2 — What You Don't Know

1. Ask a friend to share a problem with you.

2. As the friend shares the problem, write down everything you **don't** know.

3. Resist reacting with advice, judgments, emotional reactions — even if asked!

4. After 15 minutes, discuss the feelings both had during the first 15 minutes.

5. Did you avoid stereotypes and preconceptions? Did you get the whole story?

Source: Schein, E.H. (1999). *Processing consultation revisited: Building the helping relationship*. Reading, MA: Addison-Wesley OD Series. (p.41).

Active Inquiry

An essential part of Schein's PC practice model is the use of Active Inquiry. A guiding assumption in Active Inquiry is that an insecure client will not reveal essential facts about the organization's situation. Without these essential facts, the OC consultant is placed in a position of guessing. The consultant is then forced to rely on the dubious practice of projecting his or her prior experiences into the client's current situation.

There are four essential elements in Active Inquiry:

1. Build up the client's status and confidence.

2. Gather as much information as possible.

3. Involve the client in the diagnosis.

4. Create a situation that is safe for sharing both facts and feelings.

Schein describes three levels of Active Inquiry: pure inquiry, exploratory/diagnostic inquiry, and "confrontive" inquiry. It is important for the OC consultant to use the appropriate level at particular points in the process. The type of data being sought should determine the level of inquiry.

Pure inquiry, the first level, is designed to stimulate full disclosure. The consultant is simply attempting to get the story in as factual a manner as possible. At this level, "who" and "when" questions are appropriate; "why" questions are not.

Exploratory/diagnostic inquiry, the second level, is appropriate after the whole "factual" story is recorded. The consultant now redirects the client's focus with questions such as:

"How did you feel about that?"

"Why do you suppose he/she did that?"

"What are you going to do next?"

Exploratory/diagnostic inquiry gets the client to explore at a deeper level. At this level, feelings, hypotheses, cause and effect relationships, and forecasted actions can be discussed. This level reveals organizational and client member expectations, perceptions, and values.

"Confrontive" (not "confrontational") inquiry, the third level, must not occur before pure inquiry or exploratory/diagnostic inquiry. At this level, the consultant interjects his/her ideas about the situation. The goal here is to move the client members from unproductive thinking to creative and critical thinking about the current situation.

EXERCISE 3.3 — Levels of Active Inquiry

1. Ask a friend or colleague to tell you a story about something that happened to him/her recently.

2. As the "client's" story begins, make a conscious effort to ask only pure inquiry questions.

3. Become aware internally how frequently you are tempted to ask "why" questions.

4. Make a point **not** to shift to diagnostic or confrontive questions until you sense you have the "facts" of the story. (Suggestion — gently bite your lip)

5. Then, make an internal decision to shift to diagnostic/exploratory questions. Observe the impact.

6. When appropriate, shift to confrontive questions. Observe the impact.

7. After about 15 minutes, discuss the thoughts and feelings of both parties during the first 15 minutes.

Source: Schein, E.H. (1999). *Processing consultation revisited: Building the helping relationship*. Reading, MA: Addison-Wesley OD Series. (p.63).

Appreciative Inquiry

One more form of inquiry needs to be mentioned before we move on. Cooperrider and Srivastva (1987) speak of "appreciative inquiry."

Unfortunately, appreciative inquiry is often painted as a Polyanna-ish approach, in which the consultant and client look only for good things in the organization. But in practice, appreciative inquiry provides a realistic and balanced view of the organization.

In most OC engagements, the consultant enters an organization that is experiencing high levels of frustration and perhaps a sense of failure. The negative tone frequently leads to an overly pessimistic viewpoint. Appreciative inquiry helps to balance the negative threats with positive opportunities. Appreciative inquiry questions seek to record examples of what the organization is doing right. Every organization has weaknesses; every organization has strengths. The OC consultant should help client members maintain a realistic view of their organization. Schein (1999) includes appreciative inquiry as part of his PC model (p.56).

Speaking of Change

Clients "frame" their problems and possible solutions with metaphors or vocabulary of their choosing (typically, the choice is unconscious). The choice of these metaphors reveals much about the client's values and mindset. The consultant should be aware of the client's way of looking at his or her problems. Marshak (1993) discusses several possible metaphors that clients use to talk about change. I have added to, and modified, Marshak's list:

1. Engineering
2. Chemical
3. Agricultural
4. Medical
5. Cognitive
6. Spiritual
7. Sociological

The engineering mindset includes terms such as fixing, building, and redesigning. Client members using a chemical mindset speak in terms of mixing people, "good chemistry," and finding a catalyst. The agricultural terminology includes planting seeds, watering, pruning, and providing nutrients. The medical mindset looks for cures, imagines ways to inoculate, and plans to operate on or excise the cancer. The cognitive approach looks for mental maps, conceptual models, and new insights. The spiritual approach involves transcending the problem, rebirth, or conversion. The sociological speaks in terms of systems, culture, or organizational climate.

I recommend that OC consultants **not** attempt to change the client's metaphors initially. It is more important to get on the same wavelength first. Choice of vocabulary reveals valuable information about the client. Personally, I have seen the engineering mindset used rather consistently in business organizations. The "fix it" mentality dominates most of these organizations.

Relationship Building with Client Members

The goal of PC is to build an open and honest relationship, in which both facts and feelings can be shared. The client has essential information about the organization and the "problem." The consultant does not know the organization's culture or what interventions will work in that culture.

Status equilibration is a necessity in the PC model. Advantages of building a relationship of equal partners include:

1. Diagnostic insights make sense to both the consultant and the client because they are speaking the same language.

2. Solutions, in the form of interventions, are realistic for the organization's culture.

3. Evaluations of the outcomes are based on objectives that were jointly determined by the consultant and the client.

This relationship of trust must be extended to client members beyond the organizational contact. OC consultants naturally have a sense of loyalty to the organizational contact. It was the contact who "stuck out his/her neck" by recommending the consultant.

But the OC consultant must also be aware of the interests of other organizational stakeholders. There are three types of stakeholders to consider: immediate clients, hostile parties, and unsuspecting stakeholders. The immediate client members are obvious; they are involved in interviews, meetings, and other activities. Hostile parties are part of the resisting forces in Lewin's Forcefield Model. These "turf guards" are concerned about loss of power and benefits. They can derail the OC intervention. The final group is the unsuspecting stakeholders. They may or may not have political power but they should always be considered, at least for ethical reasons. The OC consultant must have the political savvy to navigate through dangerous political situations.

Face Work

In building an effective relationship with the client, Schein (1999) recommends the use of "face work" (pp.109-116). The concept of "saving face" originated in Asian societies, but is applicable in OC interventions throughout the world.

Frequently, a client feels "one down" when a consultant is hired. The client may feel that the hiring of the consultant indicates his or her inability to deal with the problem. This sense of inadequacy (feeling "one down") on the part of the client must be quickly overcome in order to establish a collaborative working relationship.

At the beginning of an OC engagement, a client with "exposed face" will have difficulty being open and honest with the consultant. Fear of humiliation will motivate defensive behavior.

In this situation, the consultant must "grant face" to the client. This can be done three ways:

1. By assuring the client that his or her input is essential to the success of any intervention.

2. By assuring the client that it's common for organizations to have such problems.

3. By sharing successes of similar organizations with similar problems.

As long as the client feels one down, the OC consultant cannot do his or her work effectively. Frequently, clients do not reveal the real problem at first because of embarrassment. It is difficult for client members to discuss their supposed or perceived failures with a complete stranger. OC consultants must earn their clients' trust.

The Role of Perceptions

It is important for the OC consultant to realize he/she is working with the client's perceptions (not "hard reality" that can be empirically proven). Human beings are constantly processing data and forming perceptions. Individuals simultaneously gather data, interpret data, and react to data.

While it appears that the steps involved in processing data are instantaneous, the steps are slowed down and explained in the work of Albert Ellis, a cognitive psychologist. Ellis and Dryden (1987) reject the S-R (stimulus-response) model of the behavioral psychologists as being overly simplistic for human beings. Ellis offers an A-B-C model:

A　Activating Event (stimulus)

B　Belief about the Activating Event

C　Consequential Thinking and/or Behavior (response)

Clearly, Ellis is adding a step (the "B" step) to the old stimulus-response model. Ellis insists it is the belief about the stimulus (not the stimulus itself) that leads to a particular response.

How we (consultants) would react to a certain stimulus is irrelevant. What is important is how the client perceives the stimulus. His/her perception is determined by his/her values, beliefs, expectations, and assumptions.

Schein's Ten Principles

Schein (1999) offers ten guiding principles for our success as OC practitioners:

1. Be Helpful — If we can't help with the particular problem, we should recommend somebody who can.
2. Remain in Touch with Current Reality — Be aware of what is going on in yourself, the client, and the system.
3. "Access Your Ignorance" — Get in the habit of writing down what

you don't know. Then, ask questions.

4. Everything You Do Is an Intervention — Everything you do influences the client.

5. The Client Owns the Problem and the Solution — The consultant does not have to live with the problem or the solution. The client does.

6. Go with the Flow — Identify the client's own areas of motivation and readiness for change.

7. Timing Is Crucial — Remain diagnostic. Look for the right time for the most appropriate intervention.

8. Be Constructively Opportunistic — Seize the teachable moment. Be ready to provide new insights and alternatives.

9. Everything Is a Source of Data and Insight — Even errors can provide valuable insight into a client's situation.

10. When in Doubt, Share the Problem — Give up the expert role. When confused, share the problem with the client.

Entry and Contracting

The OC consultant-client relationship begins with the Entry and Contracting Phase. This occurs before the six steps of the Action Research Model begin.

Typically, the OC consultant receives a phone call or letter from a potential client who describes the "presenting problem," which is the client's assessment of the problem. This is valuable input, but it must be checked out during the data gathering, feedback, and diagnostic steps of the Action Research Model.

Frequently, the client will request an educational intervention. Many potential OC clients hope a one-day workshop on one of the following topics will solve their problems:

1. leadership

2. communication

3. decision making

4. team building

While every OC intervention has a training and development (T&D) aspect, OC interventions are experiential. OC interventions usually involve short (10 minute) "mini lectures," but they do not focus on education. Most of the groups I have worked with already "know" what to do; they need to apply the knowledge. T&D interventions focus on acquiring knowledge; OC interventions focus on applying knowledge. This distinction may have to be explained to the client.

I strongly believe the OC consultant must establish the nature of the relationship immediately. In addition to discussing fees, the consultant should explain that OC work is:

1. Intrusive by nature. (The consultant will be on-site and in everybody's "business.")

2. Collaborative. (The consultant and client will jointly diagnose, design and implement interventions, and evaluate the outcomes of interventions.)

3. Time consuming. (Attempts to change an organization's systems, culture, or processes involve considerable amounts of time and effort.)

A first face-to-face meeting should be planned to determine if the OC consultant can help the client. The goal of the first meeting should be a written Problem Statement and a Preliminary Plan for Data Gathering and Feedback.

Before the first meeting, I usually send the client copies of my publications to give him or her a better idea of what to expect during an OC engagement. I make it clear to the client that either party can terminate the relationship at any time.

If the first meeting results in an agreement that I **cannot** help, I bill the client for any expenses incurred and recommend another consultant. If it is agreed that I can help, the client and I jointly write a Problem Statement and a Preliminary Plan for Data Gathering and Feedback.

Leading Versus Facilitating

Before we look at the first step in the Action Research Model, our practice model, we need to discuss the critical OC consulting role of coaching/educating senior management about the change process itself. Chapter 4 is devoted to how to coach and educate senior managers about the process of change.

REFERENCES

Cooperrider, D. & Srivastva, S. (1987). Appreciative inquiry in organizational life. In R. Woodman & W. Pasmore (Eds.), *Research in organizational change and development*, Vol.1. Greenwich, CT: JAI Press. (pp.129-169).

Ellis, A. & Dryden, W. (1987). *The practice of rational-emotive therapy*. New York: Springer Publishing.

Marshak, R.J. (1993). Managing the metaphors of change. *Organizational Dynamics*, Summer.

Schein, E.H. (1999). *Process consultation revisited: Building the helping relationship*. Reading, MA: Addison-Wesley.

CHAPTER 4

Leading Versus Facilitating Change

One of the most important roles of the OC consultant is based upon his or her expertise in the *process* of change itself. The OC consultant must be able to coach and educate senior managers in how the process of change takes place in organizations.

Change is a process that follows a relatively predictable pattern. Unfortunately, many managers (including CEOs) have never been educated about the change process. It should come as no surprise that leading change without knowledge of the change process itself typically leads to failure of the change effort.

This lack of senior management understanding of the change process itself creates one of the most important roles for the OC consultant — Change Process Advisor/Educator. The OC consultant should be prepared to advise/educate senior managers on how to effectively lead change.

Leading change is **not** the role of the OC consultant. Leading change is the responsibility of the company's senior management. The OC consultant should serve senior managers as an advisor/educator and coach.

In the first part of this chapter we will look at the steps in effectively leading change. The second part of this chapter will discuss other issues that are crucial for effectively implementing change.

Steps in Leading Change

For our purposes in this book we will not get involved in the debate over how many actual steps there are in the change process. Various experts disagree — many with strong arguments.

For our purpose of advising/educating managers on how to effectively lead change, lets follow Kotter's (1996) model of eight steps:

1. Establish a sense of urgency.
2. Create a guiding coalition.
3. Develop vision and strategy for the specific change.
4. Communicate the change vision and strategic plan.
5. Empower employees for action.
6. Generate short-term wins.
7. Consolidate gains and produce more change.
8. Anchor the new changes in the culture.

Let's take a closer look at each step.

1) Establish a Sense of Urgency

I agree with Kotter (1996) that the first step in a change effort is to establish a sense of urgency. Managers are busy people. To get the attention and commitment of the organizational managers, the change leader must convince these busy managers of the importance, the urgency, for the change.

Kotter (1996) states, "With urgency low, it's difficult to put together a group with enough power and credibility to guide the effort or convince key individuals to spend the time necessary to create and communicate a change vision" (p.36). Even with the leadership of the best CEO, "if many others don't feel the same sense of urgency, the momentum for change will probably die far short of the finish line" (p.36).

Senior management, with the guidance of the OC consultant, should consider ways to counteract what Kotter (1996) calls "sources of complacency." In his book he lists the following nine reasons for complacency:

1. the absence of a major and visible crisis
2. too many visible resources
3. low overall performance standards
4. organizational structures with narrow functional goals
5. measurement of the wrong performance indexes

6. lack of feedback from external sources

7. a "kill-the-messenger-of-bad-news" culture

8. denial of problems

9. too much "happy talk" from senior management

Kotter (1996) offers this valuable reminder, "never underestimate the magnitude of the forces that reinforce complacency and that help maintain the status quo." Remember our discussion of Lewin's Forcefield Analysis in Chapter 2? Every situation (the current status quo) is supported by resisting forces.

Raising the urgency level involves senior management responding to each of the nine sources of complacency. Let me suggest the following direct responses to each one in order:

1. Provide "visuals" of what will happen without the change.

2. Sell the corporate jet; close the executive dining hall.

3. Establish "stretch" goals for everybody in the organization.

4. Create cross-function teams with cross-functional goals.

5. Re-evaluate how the organization measures "success" (what gets measured by senior management gets employee attention).

6. Actively seek feedback from external sources (customers, industry analysts, etc.).

7. Reward the messenger who has the courage to reveal problems.

8. Openly discuss organizational weaknesses.

9. Have senior managers demonstrate realistic, problem-confronting communication.

2) Create a Guiding Coalition

Over the past few decades, we have created mythological heroic characters out of successful CEOs (similar to the myths about military heroes in earlier societies). CEOs such as Jack Welch (GE), Lee Iacocca (Chrysler), Sam Walton (Wal-Mart), and Lou Gerstner (IBM) deserve a lot of credit for their accomplishments. But the heroics of a single person are not enough to lead tens of thousands of employees.

Senior management must create a strong coalition of organizational leaders to guide the change effort.

The issue here is not executive knowledge. I have met some extremely knowledgeable executives. The issue here is "buy-in." Without buy-in from key players, the change effort will fail.

Kotter (1996) suggests four key member characteristics for effective coalitions:

1. position power — the coalition needs key players, including board members and line managers
2. expertise and diversity — the coalition needs the expertise and diversity necessary to make informed, intelligent decisions
3. credibility — the coalition must have the credibility, based on the members' reputations, to be taken seriously
4. leadership — the coalition must have proven leaders (p.57)

Kotter (1996) also suggests qualities to avoid; people to keep **off** the team. He recommends avoiding big egos and "snakes."

Big egos can destroy a talented and committed coalition. Members of the coalition must be talented leaders who have a realistic sense of their own limitations. Kotter (1996) believes "egos that fill the room leave no space for anybody else" (p.59). Effective teamwork is impossible when a few over-inflated egos dominate the team.

"Snakes" undermine the work of the coalition. Snakes can destroy the trust that is essential for a strong, influential coalition.

The change agent must have a team (coalition) of committed leaders leading the change effort in each team. These team leaders must pass along essential information to organizational members. Team leaders must immediately confront rumors and provide inspiration for their teams. These leaders must "know how to encourage people to transcend short-term parochial interests" (Kotter, 1996, p.65).

3) Develop a Vision & Strategy for the Specific Change
Every organization should already have a clear vision and a well-crafted

strategic plan. If not, please refer to Chapter 7. (These are **not** the issues here.)

When leading a specific change effort, it is important to develop a vision and strategy for that **specific** change. The fact that this is step 3, instead of step 1, is significant.

No leader, regardless of talent, should single-handedly develop the vision and strategy for the specific change effort. Even if the leader is capable of developing a grand vision and a well-crafted strategic plan, the more important issue here is buy-in.

The change leader should actively elicit participation from all of the coalition members. This participation provides valuable input into the decision-making process, plus it gives the coalition members a sense of ownership in the plan.

The vision for the specific change effort must inspire organizational members. A vision makes decision making easier by eliminating many of the possible distracters. A shared vision is helpful throughout the organization. Kotter (1996) states, "With clarity of vision, managers and employees can figure out for themselves what to do without constantly checking with a boss or their peers" (p.70).

Kotter (1996) believes the following six characteristics should be present in an effective vision:

1. imaginable
2. desirable
3. feasible
4. focused
5. flexible
6. communicable

An imaginable and desirable vision paints a picture of a very appealing future. Kotter (1996) correctly states the vision must "appeal to most of the people who have a stake in the enterprise: employees, customers, stockholders, suppliers, community" (p.73). Obviously, you cannot please all the people, all the time. But the vision and strategic development process should, at least, consider the long-term interests of all stakeholders. If groups of stakeholders believe they are forced to make unreasonable sacrifices, resistance to change may be insurmountable.

Feasibility is a crucial issue in any vision or strategic plan. Ambitious goals must be doable. "Stretch" goals are motivating, but unrealistic goals actually de-motivate. Employees don't buy-in, and they lose respect for management.

Focus and flexibility represent a delicate balance. The focus must be narrow enough to harness limited resources (time, energy, and money), but flexible enough to take advantage of peripheral opportunities. The vision and strategic plan have to be adaptable to a changing environment.

Lastly, an effective vision must be communicable. This characteristic is so important, Kotter (1996) devotes an entire chapter to it. We will briefly discuss it next.

4) Communicate the Change Vision & Strategic Plan

A group vision and well-crafted strategic plan is of little value if it sits on a shelf gathering dust. The value of the vision and strategic plan is the guidance they provide in goal setting and decision making. To provide guidance they must be communicated throughout the organization.

Kotter (1996) warns managers about "undercommunicating" and sending "inconsistent messages." Senior managers must think beyond communicating to only their immediate subordinates. A plan must be developed to communicate the vision and strategic plan to everybody in the organization.

Kotter (1996) believes undercommunication frequently happens because the communication of the vision gets lost in "a river of routine communication" (p.88). Employees get distracted by hundreds of messages that appear important or urgent. Frequently, these distracters obscure the truly important. Kotter (1996, p.89) estimates only about 1/2 of 1% of most company communication is devoted to the vision.

Kotter (1996) offers the following suggestions for effectively communicating the vision:

1. simplicity
2. metaphor, analogy, and example
3. multiple forums
4. repetition
5. leadership by example
6. explanation of seeming inconsistencies
7. give-and-take

Let's take a look at each suggestion.

Simplicity means avoiding jargon and technobabble. Employees will not be inspired by a vision they don't understand. A metaphor, analogy, or example provides a picture.

Multiple forums and repetition are crucial for successful communication of the vision. The vision should be communicated through training sessions, meetings, memos, press releases, the company's intranet, etc. Repetition, through the various forums, is necessary to make the message stick.

Leading by example is very important. In fact, it is difficult to lead by only talking-the-talk. If senior managers don't walk-the-walk, employees will not take the message seriously.

While leading by example, managers will invariably have to exhibit some apparently inconsistent behaviors. Any apparent inconsistencies must be addressed, if management hopes to maintain the credibility of the vision.

Finally, give-and-take is necessary to maintain an open, interactive organizational culture. Senior managers should actively solicit feedback and make adjustments as necessary.

5) *Empower Employees for Broad-Based Action*

Empowering employees is based on the leadership principle called path-goal theory. Path-goal (perhaps, more accurately goal-path) leadership style starts with establishing a goal with the employee. Then, the leader's remaining responsibility is to help clear the path so that the employee can accomplish the goal. Empowering the employee is dramatically different from the management style of micromanaging and controlling.

In this new management style, managers serve as facilitators. Managers work to acquire the resources their employees need to reach their goals. These resources could include time, money, personnel, or training.

Kotter (1996) states, "new behavior, skills, and attitudes will be needed when major changes are initiated" (p.108). Satisfying these needs may require considerable training.

Empowering employees may require dramatic changes in HR policies (selection, compensation, performance evaluation, promotion criteria, etc.). HR policies must support the development of an empowered workforce.

Employee empowerment may also require changes in management. The command-and-control management style must go. If these old-style managers cannot be retrained, they must be dismissed. Kotter (1996) correctly states, [if] "others see that these people are not being confronted…they become discouraged" (p.114).

6) Generate Short-Term Wins

Executives who have ignored this step have paid with their jobs (or careers!). Business leaders, especially in the U.S., look for short-term results. While it is important to have long-term plans for success, no change agent should ignore the importance of providing some short-term wins.

Remember, anytime a change agent is leading change there are resisting forces and driving forces. It is important to keep the driving forces committed to the cause. All managers are under pressure to present short-term wins. Therefore, the coalition managers must have something to show.

These short-term wins do not necessarily need to be earthshaking. But they need to be big enough to inspire the driving forces and to silence the resisting forces. Short-term wins build the credibility of the plan for change.

Kotter (1996, pp.121-22) lists three characteristics for good short-term wins:

1. it's visible
2. it's unambiguous
3. it's clearly related to the change effort

Short-term wins, with these three characteristics, should be woven into the timetable for the change effort. Kotter (1996) recommends "six months" for small companies, and "eighteen months" for big organizations.

Short-term wins let organizational members know that the sacrifices are worth it. These wins also "turn neutrals into supporters" (Kotter, 1996, p.123). It is important to build and maintain momentum for the change effort.

Kotter (1996) offers the following general rule: "the more cynics and resisters, the more important are short-term wins" (p.123). Kotter goes on to say, "short-term pressure can be a useful way to keep up the urgency rate" (p.127). It is important to maintain the urgency established in step 1.

7) Consolidate Gains and Produce More Change

In this step, after some short-term wins, managers must continue to diligently monitor the progress of the change effort. Remember, the resisting forces are "waiting for an opportunity to make a comeback. Whenever you let up before the job is done, critical momentum can be lost and regression may follow." (Kotter, 1996, p.133).

This is a good time to revisit Kurt Lewin's Forcefield Analysis. Re-evaluate the current scenario. What or who are the resisting forces now? What or who are the current driving forces? Current circumstances may call for a new plan to build support. Perhaps it's time to expand the guiding coalition.

Kotter (1996) believes, "the credibility afforded by the short-term wins [can be used to] push forward faster, tackling even more or bigger projects" (p.140).

During large transformation efforts, multiple changes may be taking place at the same time. It may be necessary to sequence these changes to maximize the use of resources (time, energy, and money). The guiding coalition members should contribute and "buy-in" to this sequencing or scheduling of events.

This step requires senior management's best efforts to not only maintain but also to build momentum for the change.

8) *Anchor the New Change in the Culture*

Kotter's (1996) eighth step is the same thing Kurt Lewin called "refreezing" in his Three-Step Model of Change. Once positive change happens, management must work to make it part of the organizational culture.

The new organizational culture must be reinforced by the policies for recruiting, selecting, promoting, compensating, evaluating, and training. We will discuss organizational culture change in detail in Chapter 9.

Power and Politics

Political Savvy

It is a fact of organizational life: politics influence virtually everything that happens in an organization. Leaders, especially change leaders, must develop political savvy. I am **not** advocating unethical behavior, but I am recommending that leaders consciously fine tune their political awareness.

Organizations continuously experience different individuals, groups, and coalitions vying for scarce resources. Each one is attempting to maintain or enhance its self interests. Many leaders, and OC consultants, underestimate these powerful forces.

Any attempt to implement organizational change will invariably threaten one of these individuals, groups, or coalitions. Organizational change is frequently accompanied by conflicting interests, unethical behavior, and emotional turmoil. Change leaders must learn to navigate these dangerous waters.

Power and Change

The word "power" has positive and negative connotations. In this chapter, we will concentrate on the positive, ethical uses of power. Burke (1982) believes "for change to occur in an organization, power must be exercised" (p.127).

Let's take a brief look at Richard Emerson's Power-Dependency Theory. Emerson's (1962) theory depicts a social relationship between two parties in which scarce resources (commodities and rewards) are controlled by one party and desired by another. Thus, power is inherent in any social relationship in which one person depends on another.

"Commodities" in power-dependency theory can include social commodities, such as respect, praise, influence, and information. French and Bell (1999) state, "We enter into and continue in exchange relationships when what we receive from others is equivalent to or in excess of what we must give to others" (p.284).

Bases of Power

Managers and OC consultants should be able to recognize the bases of power individuals, groups, and coalitions exert in organizations.

French and Raven (1959) suggest five bases of power:

1. reward power — based on the ability to reward another
2. coercive power — based on the ability to punish another
3. legitimate power — based on the holder's position
4. referent power — based on charisma (i.e. popularity)
5. expert power — based on knowledge or expertise

Mintzberg (1983) also speaks of five bases of power:

1. control of a critical resource
2. control of a critical technical skill
3. control of a critical body of knowledge

4. legal prerogatives (e.g., exclusive rights)
5. access to any of the other four bases

Additionally, Mintzberg believed the influencer must have both the "will and skill" to use his or her base(s) of power.

Salancik and Pfeffer (1977) also contribute some valuable insights into our understanding of power in organizational settings. They view power as a positive and necessary force for change and progress in organizations. They believe power bases can be created by the placement of allies in key positions.

Using Political/Power Skills

For change efforts to succeed, managers/change agents must develop and use power skills. The first skill required is the ability to analyze the current political situation. Failure in this assessment phase invariably leads to frustrated change efforts.

French and Bell (1999) believe, "one gains a quick understanding of the overall political climate of an organization by studying its methods of resource allocation, conflict resolution, and choosing among alternative means and goals" (p.286).

Greiner and Schein (1988) believe change agents must be able to assess their own power and to identify key stakeholders. Only after assessing their own power base(s) can they determine how to use it/ them to influence others. This assessment will also reveal areas where enhancement of power is necessary. Some of these weak areas can be strengthened by developing allies in the organization.

Beer (1980, pp.258-261) suggests the following:

1. demonstrate competence
2. cultivate multiple relationships with key power figures
3. acquire multiple top-level sponsors
4. score early successes for credibility
5. gain control of valuable resources
6. work toward group support

French and Bell (1999) believe the following "rules of thumb are implied by the fact that power accrues to persons who control valued resources or commodities" (pp.292-294):

1. become a desired commodity — competent and trustworthy person and professional

2. make the OC program itself a commodity — demonstrate how it adds strategic advantage to the organization

3. serve the needs of multiple people and groups

4. create win-win solutions

5. help the managers (the sponsors) succeed

6. be an expert at process, not content

7. fulfill the role of facilitator

Managing the Transition

Organizational change plans are rarely accomplished in one quick step. Implementation usually requires senior managers who can lead the organization through a transition period.

Beckhard and Harris (1987) discuss three major activities and structures to lead the transition: activity planning, commitment planning, and change-management structures.

Activity planning "involves making a road map for change, citing specific activities and events that must occur if the transition is to be successful" (Cummings & Worley, 2001). Activity planning should receive participation from all key stakeholders. Achievable, incremental goals should be identified on the "road map."

While it is important that activity planning be well thought out, the plan must be adaptable enough to react to the feedback received during the transition. A successful transition will include both proactive and reactive decisions. Activity planning should provide the general direction for efforts during the transition period.

Commitment planning involves "identifying key people and groups whose commitment is needed for change to occur" (Cummings & Worley, 2001). Commitment planning should be done early. Commitment is essential from those who can wield influence and control resources.

Change-management structures for the transition period can help provide needed direction and security for this frequently turbulent time. Members of major constituencies should play major roles during the transition.

Sustaining Momentum

The initial excitement generated by the planned change is often squelched by the first few frustrating roadblocks. Cummings and Worley (2001) correctly state, "A strong tendency exists among organizational members to return to what is learned and well known unless they receive sustained support and reinforcement for carrying the changes through to completion" (p.168).

Cummings and Worley (2001) list the following five activities for change leaders to sustain momentum:

1. providing resources for change
2. building a support system for change agents
3. developing new competencies and skills
4. reinforcing new behaviors
5. staying the course

Let's take a brief look at each activity.

Implementing change often requires substantial resources (time, money, and human resources). Change leaders must devote considerable time and effort to acquire these resources. Organizational members typically underestimate the amount of resources required to implement a change. Worley, Hitchin, and Ross (1996) recommend a separate "change budget" earmarking resources for training and other needs.

A support system for change agents is very important. A system of mutual learning and emotional support for the change agents should not be ignored. Cummings and Worley (2001, p.170) recommend using "trusted colleagues as 'shadow consultants' to help think through difficult issues with clients and to offer conceptual and emotional support."

Developing new competencies and skills is essential in every OC effort. Cummings and Worley (2001) recommend the use of "traditional training programs, on-the-job counseling and coaching, and experiential simulations, covering both technical and social skills" (p.170).

Reinforcing new behaviors provides the rewards individuals need for their continuing efforts. Management can use extrinsic or intrinsic rewards, as long as the rewards are valuable to the recipients.

Like the captain of a ship, change leaders must lead through stormy seas before the rewards of change are obtained. Change leaders must remain focused on the goal and be able to inspire those who get discouraged. It's hard work, but it's worth it!

Now that we have looked at the change process itself, and at how to coach senior management on what to expect during that process, let's move on to data gathering. Data gathering, the first step in the Action Research Model, will be the topic of Chapter 5.

REFERENCES

Beckhard, R. & Harris, R. (1987). *Organizational transitions: Managing complex change* (2nd ed.). Reading, MA: Addison-Wesley.

Beer, M. (1980). *Organizational change and development: A systems view.* Santa Monica, CA: Goodyear.

Burke, W.W. (1982). *Organization development: Principles and practices.* Boston: Little, Brown, & Co.

Cummings, T.G. & Worley, C.G. (2001). *Organization development and change* (7th ed.). Cincinnati, OH: South-Western.

Emerson, R.M. (1962). Power-dependence relations. *American Sociological Review, 27,* pp.31-40.

French, J.R.P. & Raven, B. (1959). The bases of social power. In D. Cartwright (Ed.), *Studies in social power.* Ann Arbor, MI: Institute for Social Research, University of Michigan. (pp.150-167).

French, W.L. & Bell, C.H., Jr. (1999). *Organization development* (6th ed.). Upper Saddle River, NJ: Prentice-Hall.

Greiner, L.E. & Schein, V.E. (1988). *Power and organization development: Mobilizing power to implement change.* Reading, MA: Addison-Wesley.

Kotter, J.P. (1996). *Leading change*. Boston, MA: Harvard Business School Press.

Mintzberg, H. (1983). *Power in and around organizations*. Englewood Cliffs, NJ: Prentice-Hall. (pp.24-26).

Salancik, G. & Pfeffer, J. (1977). Who gets power — and how they hold on to it: A strategic-contingency model of power. *Organizational Dynamics*, 5, p.3.

Worley, C., Hitchin, D., & Ross, W. (1996). *Integrated strategic change: How OD helps build competitive advantage*. Reading, MA: Addison-Wesley.

CHAPTER 5

Data Gathering

Data gathering, feedback, and diagnosis (the first three steps in the Action Research Model) are the focus of chapters five and six. Of course, some preliminary data gathering, feedback, and diagnosis took place during the initial meeting with the client. Now, after the completion of the Entry and Contracting Phase, the OC consultant must conduct a systematic and thorough analysis of the client's situation.

The first step in the Action Research Model is data gathering. In workshops I have conducted for OC practitioners, I have said, "Data gathering is the most important step in the Action Research Model." After receiving a few skeptical looks, I explain why. Gathering the proper data leads to a proper diagnosis; proper diagnosis leads to the choice of a proper intervention.

In our discussion of data gathering, we must look at both methods and targets. OC consultants must pick the appropriate methods to gather the needed data, and the data gathering must focus on the appropriate targets. First, we will look at six data gathering methods. Then, we will look at six target groups and six target processes.

Six Data Gathering Methods

There are basically six data gathering methods available to OC practitioners:

1. questionnaires
2. interviews
3. observations
4. company document reviews
5. psychological instruments
6. anonymous letter writing
7. Group Assessment Method 55

All of these methods have strengths and weaknesses. No single method is always appropriate. I recommend using more than one method, whenever possible. If data from the various methods are consistent, the confidence level of the diagnosis is elevated. If data from the various methods are inconsistent, diagnostic conclusions are questionable.

Questionnaires provide fixed responses to a set of pre-determined questions. They are easily administered to large numbers of organizational members and are quickly analyzed due to the Likert-type (one to five or seven) structure of the responses. Large numbers of participants is the advantage. Disadvantages include the forced nature of the responses and the possibility of asking the "wrong" questions.

Interviews are perhaps the most widely used method of gathering data in OC. Interviews provide for a more in-depth exploration of issues. While interviewing is time consuming and expensive (in terms of opportunity costs), it allows for the building of rapport between consultant and client. Group interviews, after individual interviews, further add to the richness of this data.

Interviews can be highly structured, highly unstructured, or somewhere in between. Highly structured interviews yield little more "depth" than questionnaires, while being far more time consuming. Highly unstructured interviews yield "rich" and interesting data, but the data is difficult to compare from interviewee to interviewee.

Observations provide data on actual behavior rather than reported behavior. While this approach initially sounds more objective, observations are fraught with interpretation difficulties. For example, if I observe one meeting (or two), have I seen "typical" behavior? Are client member biases simply being replaced by my biases? Most importantly, observations cannot answer the "why" question. Typically, observations will have to be used along with other methods.

Company documents (such as financial reports, budgets, organization charts, grievances, minutes of meetings, correspondence with customers and suppliers) are free from client member and consultant biases. Reviewing these company documents provides valuable insight into the organization's structure, operating procedures, and priorities for resources. This method is limited but helpful.

Psychological instruments (also called personality inventories or preference instruments) provide insight into individual preferences and group dynamics. Numerous instruments are available at reasonable prices. I recommend **not** using any of the cheap imitations found on the internet. Use only instruments that have undergone rigorous validity and reliability testing.

The choice of psychological instruments should be determined by the type of data the consultant wishes to gather. Instruments are available for gathering data on introversion/extraversion; needs for inclusion, control, and openness; communication styles; learning preferences, and more.

Several organizations help OC practitioners use psychological instruments. One organization I have used is High Performing Systems (**www.hpsys.com**) in Norcross, Georgia. Dr. Dick Thompson and his associates provide training, certification, and support on the following instruments:

1. Myers-Briggs Type Indicator
2. FIRO Elements B
3. The Communication Wheel
4. ABLE (for 360 degree feedback)

Anonymous letter writing can be used in many situations, but it is especially helpful in situations where client members fear retaliation for negative comments. Many organizations have "sacred cows," problem people or issues that go unchallenged. The OC consultant must address the organization's dysfunctional, counterproductive sacred cows.

Six Target Groups

There are six target groups and six target processes for data gathering and diagnosis. Let's look at the six target groups first:

1. Entire Organization
2. Large Subsystem

3. Group/Team

4. Intergroup

5. Dyads

6. Individual Members or Roles   7 Group Assessment Method.

The target group for data gathering and diagnosis will dictate which data gathering methods are appropriate. What is appropriate at the entire organization or large subsystem level may not be appropriate at the dyad or individual level.

Entire Organization

When the entire organization is the target, all six data gathering methods are available, but some are more appropriate than others. Questionnaires are extremely useful at the entire organization level. Questionnaires are designed for large numbers of participants, the situation encountered at this level. Even though the amount of data collected will be very large, the consultant can quickly summarize and analyze the responses.

Interviewing the entire organization is impossible, for practical reasons, but selective interviews with senior managers or key personnel are possible and highly recommended.

Observations, like interviews, can be used selectively at the entire organization level. Observing a few meetings can quickly give the OC consultant a sense of the organization's culture.

Document review at this level is very valuable. Mission statements, strategic plans, policy manuals, budgets, and minutes of board meetings provide considerable insight into organizations.

Psychological instruments, unless used selectively, are inappropriate at this level. I believe the use of psychological instruments commits the consultant to being available for individual participant feedback and interpretation.

Anonymous letter writing can reveal many of the unspoken problems in the organization. Those self-addressed envelopes that arrive in the mail can provide the consultant with valuable insight.

Determining the appropriate data gathering method at this level (and at any other level) depends on what information is sought. At the entire organization level, we want to know:

1. Are the mission and strategy of the organization clear?
2. How do members describe the culture?
3. What are the norms and expectations?
4. Is leadership autocratic or participative?
5. Is the company an industry leader or follower?
6. Is communication direct or indirect?
7. Is the organization open or closed to new ideas?
8. Are organizational members cooperative or competitive?

Large Subsystems

Large subsystems are the major units of the organization — subsidiaries, divisions, locations, or departments. Large subsystems typically have their own purpose and structure, and they have developed their own distinct culture.

Once again, all six data gathering methods are available at this level, but some are more appropriate than others. Questionnaires work well here because they allow all the members of the subsystem to participate. Large amounts of data can be quickly analyzed.

Interviews may be difficult here for the same reason questionnaires work so well — large numbers. Keep in mind that interviews provide deeper, richer data, but comparative analysis is more difficult. If you insist on doing interviews here, do it selectively.

Observations can be helpful in discerning the unique culture of the subsystem. Document review can shed light on performance issues.

Psychological instruments can provide insight into the current leadership, communication, and decision-making styles. Anonymous letter writing will probably yield some surprises.

At this level, the OC consultant is seeking information about the following:

1. What's the purpose of the subsystem?
2. How does the subsystem view the whole?
3. How does the whole view the subsystem?
4. Are the subsystem's goals aligned with the organization's goals?
5. How do subsystem members get along?
6. What are the current problems facing the subsystem?

Group/Team

While it may sound like "academic hair splitting," there is a distinction between groups and teams. Groups are more loosely knit; the members are not highly dependent on their co-workers. On the other hand, team members are dependent on their co-workers for success. Both groups and teams typically have a common supervisor, but they vary in degrees of interdependency.

Questionnaires are less effective at the group/team level because of smaller numbers of participants. The responses of very small group/teams may show little consistency; therefore, they are difficult to interpret.

Interviews are quite valuable at this target level. In addition to gathering information, they allow for the building of rapport with individual client members. Likewise, observations of group/team meetings will reveal much about group dynamics. Document review at this level involves performance evaluations and group/team reports to supervisors.

Psychological instruments are a great way to gather data about member preferences. Sharing this data with the group/team during the feedback session is usually well received, in my experience. I will say more about this in the Feedback part of the next chapter.

Anonymous letter writing is less effective at the group/team level because members doubt their responses are truly anonymous.

Information sought from the group/team includes:

1. Are members cooperative or competitive?
2. Are member-leader relationships satisfactory?

3. What are the major problems facing the group/team?

4. Do members believe they are valued by the group/team?

5. Is the group/team valued by the organization?

Intergroup

Conflict or communication problems between two or more groups can be very destructive in organizations. Diagnosis in this area is very important. What the client believes is a conflict or communication problem may have roots in unclear role expectations or perceptions. It is necessary to gather the appropriate data to properly diagnosis the problem.

Questionnaires are especially effective when dealing with large groups. This method allows all members to participate. After the questionnaires are completed, themes can be derived from the response data. Interviews are probably more appropriate for smaller groups.

Most attempts to diagnose intergroup problems will benefit from interviews. Interviewing the group leaders is usually particularly valuable. The group leaders typically can provide the history and overview of the problem. Then, subsequent interviews with key players can be planned. Conducting separate interviews with each group as a whole can also be helpful.

Observations can reveal group dynamics and patterns of behavior that the group members may be taking for granted. Some of their dysfunctional behaviors may have continued for months or years without being questioned. Unaddressed dysfunctional behaviors can become part of the culture.

Reviewing company documents will probably provide very little data. Many companies do individual employee performance evaluations on a periodic basis, but few companies conduct group/team performance evaluations. Problems with other groups may not be "documented" problems.

Psychological instruments can be beneficial here because they reveal group member preferences concerning communication, decision-making, and leadership styles. If previous team building work has been done with the separate groups, this data may already be available.

I have found anonymous letter writing to be less effective in these us-versus-them situations. Most group members have little difficulty discussing problems they perceive with other groups (them). So, this method will typically not reveal many surprises.

One popular method used with intergroup situations is the Confrontation Meeting. The Confrontation Meeting has a diagnostic component, but it is more correctly classified as an intervention. I will cover the Confrontation Meeting, in some detail, in the Intervention Part of the book.

Being clear on what information is being sought is important in this area. When the target is two or more groups, OC consultants want to know:

1. How do the groups perceive each other?
2. What does each group expect from the other?
3. Are the groups interdependent?
4. Does the reward system promote competition?

Dyads

Dyads are made up of two organizational members: supervisor and subordinate, two peers, or linking pins. Linking pins connect two or more groups or departments. What is frequently described as inter-group conflict may in fact be conflict between linking pins.

A dysfunctional dyad involving two department heads can wreak havoc in an organization. Invariably, these department heads not only create problems for their departments but for other departments as well.

Questionnaires may not work well if small numbers of organiza-tional members are involved. Interviews are almost required here. The OC consultant must understand the perceptions of the parties in the dyad.

Observations of interactions between the two parties frequently reveal dysfunctional behaviors by both parties. Document reviews (employee performance evaluations in particular) may provide third-party confirmation of the dyad problem.

Psychological instruments are very valuable here. Interpersonal conflict, communication problems, and differing expectations are frequently rooted in different preferences. Preferences are not necessarily good or bad, but they are usually strongly held.

I would recommend against anonymous letter writing here because it is difficult to keep the responses anonymous. Anonymous letter writing, like questionnaires, is more appropriate when working with large numbers of client members.

When working with dyads, OC consultants want to know the following:

1. Do the parties have the necessary people skills?
2. Do the parties know the expectations for their roles?
3. Does the system reward cooperative or competitive behavior?

Individual Members or Roles

When an individual member or role (job) is the target, a needs analysis, similar to those done by training and development (T&D) professionals, is helpful. The training needs analysis (TNA) conducted by T&D professionals compares the current KSAs (knowledge, skills, and attitudes) possessed by the individual employee with the required KSAs of the role/job (found in a job analysis). This provides rich data for the OC consultant.

Using questionnaires at the individual member or role target level is usually not appropriate, unless the individual member or role has widespread influence in the organization.

Interviews are important here because we want the individual member to participate in his or her diagnosis and action plan. Interviews with individuals about their roles can build rapport, and they generally lead to member buy-in for a particular intervention. Also, interviews conducted individually or in groups can provide needed data about role expectations.

Observations and company documents are complementary methods when individual members or roles are the target. Most companies retain employee performance evaluations for long periods of time. These evaluations should be based on the job descriptions and job specifications. Observations can confirm or disconfirm behavioral problems and possibly reveal unrealistic expectations for the role.

Psychological instruments are very useful here because they often reveal things individuals were not fully aware of themselves. These instruments are also helpful in determining job "fit" for the individual employee.

Anonymous letter writing may not be very effective here unless the individual member or role influences large numbers of organizational members.

The information sought for this target includes:

1. How does the individual evaluate him/herself?
2. How do others evaluate the individual?
3. Is the role/job adequately defined?
4. How is proper fit determined for this role/job?
5. Is proper training provided?

Six Target Processes

We have looked at the six data gathering methods and the six target groups for data gathering. Now, let's turn our focus to some crucial organizational processes. The following six organizational processes are critical for an organization to meet its financial objectives and to maintain a satisfied workforce:

1. Strategic Planning/Goal Setting
2. Leadership
3. Decision Making/Problem Solving
4. Communication Patterns

5. Conflict Management

6. Organizational Learning

Strategic Planning/Goal Setting

I believe strategic planning is the most important process in any organization. The strategic plan should drive every other process in the organization. The responsibility for a well-crafted strategic plan rests squarely on the shoulders of senior management. While we will discuss several ways to elicit input from all organizational members in the Strategic Planning Interventions chapter, senior management must take the ultimate responsibility for crafting and implementing the strategic plan.

Once the organization's strategic plan is in place, managers throughout the firm can proceed with goal setting in their areas of responsibility. Effective goal setting at the department or group level is impossible without an effective strategic plan at the entire-organization level.

We will discuss the strategic planning process and strategic change interventions in great detail in Part II of this text. At this point, we want to look at the methods OC consultants use to gather data about the organization's strategic planning and goal setting process.

Questionnaires are effective with this target process because they provide perceptions from various organizational levels and functions concerning the developing and communicating of the strategic plan. Since strategic planning and goal setting affects every organizational member, questionnaires are ideal for gathering data from large numbers of individuals.

Interviews must focus on key organizational members — selected individuals at various levels and in different functions. Observing meetings will help determine if goal setting in the organization fits into the strategic plan.

Company document review can be helpful if the company requires written goals (or strategic plans) from each department. OC consultants are looking for alignment (fit) with the organizational strategic plan.

It is not practical to give psychological instruments (and feedback) to all organizational members, but the psychological preferences of the senior management members will reveal much about the strategic plan.

Anonymous letter writing may reveal whether or not the organizational culture will support the strategic plan.

The information sought concerning the strategic planning and goal setting process includes:

1. Who participates in the strategic planning process?
2. Are the mission and strategic plan of the organization clear?
3. Do departmental goals fit the organization's strategic plan?
4. Are the strategic plan and departmental goals realistic?

Leadership

Leadership, like strategic planning, has a pervasive influence on the organization. A dogmatic, micro-managing approach initiated at the top of the organization can trickledown to the other levels of management. Fortunately, an inspiring, people-empowering leadership style at the top can also influence management throughout the organization.

Leadership is necessary to implement the organization's strategic plan. Leadership practices can inspire or demoralize the workforce.

Completed questionnaires from managers and non-managers will reveal much about the functionality or dysfunctionality of current management practices. Poor management practices have difficulty hiding from a system-wide questionnaire.

Selective interviews may be helpful to explain some of the practices revealed in questionnaires. Of course, the interviewer must guarantee the confidentiality of open and honest responses.

Observations help to confirm the concerns about management practices that are found in the questionnaires. Document reviews, performance evaluations in particular, may disclose management development needs for individual managers. Psychological instruments completed by managers provide insight into why individual managers prefer certain behaviors.

Anonymous letter writing provides a safe way for organizational members to speak out about dysfunctional management practices or particularly ineffective managers.

Information sought about leaders and leadership of the organization includes:

1. Are senior managers respected as role models?
2. Which leadership style is favored in the organization?
3. How are leaders promoted?
4. Is a formal management development program offered?
5. How are leader-subordinate disagreements handled?

Decision Making/Problem Solving

Decision making/problem solving styles tend to permeate an organization, or at least large subsystems of the organization. This continuous, day-by-day process is critical for organizational success. No matter how well-crafted the strategic plan, or how effective the management team is, all organizational members must be trained and empowered to contribute to decision making and problem solving.

Questionnaires can disclose decision-making style, who participates in decisions, how problems are solved, and how dissent is dealt with. Interview questions can be used to add depth to the responses gained through the questionnaires.

Observations and document reviews often reveal discrepancies between espoused values and actual practices concerning participation in decision making and problem solving. If meetings are dominated by one or two voices, the quality of group decision making is in doubt. Reviewing meeting minutes typically provides considerable data about decision making and problem solving in the organization.

The preferences revealed by psychological instruments will help the OC consultant understand why organizational members adopt particular decision-making or problem-solving styles. Anonymous letter writing can reveal some otherwise undisclosed decision-making and problem-solving practices.

For this target process, the following information is sought:

1. Who participates in decision making and problem solving?
2. Is group brainstorming used?
3. How are alternatives evaluated?
4. How are action plans determined?

Communication Patterns

The communication system is the central nervous system of the organization. Without this system, the various parts of the organization will not know how to respond. A coordinated effort of all organizational parts is necessary to implement the organization's strategic plan. All organizational members must be connected to the communication system.

Questionnaires are beneficial here because all members have perceptions concerning the organizational climate. Selective interviews may help explain the findings in the questionnaire responses. Observations can confirm member perceptions or provide insight into member misperceptions.

Company document reviews may reveal who is involved in communication. Documents will reveal who is privy to various types of information. Psychological instruments will reveal the communication preferences of key players.

Anonymous letter writing frequently discloses feelings of individuals being left "out of the loop." These feelings, whether real or imaginary, should be addressed by management.

When the target process is communication, OC consultants seek the following information:

1. Is the communication climate open or closed?
2. Is communication direct or indirect?
3. Is communication top-down, bottom-up, and lateral?
4. Is communication appropriate for the task/relationship?

Conflict Management

Like cholesterol, conflict comes in good forms and bad forms. The good forms of conflict (e.g., the debate over new ideas to solve old problems) can enhance an organization's productivity. The bad forms of conflict (e.g., two department heads involved in a turf war) can be highly counterproductive.

Conflict, both interpersonal and intergroup, should be managed — not eliminated! In fact, the major advantage of teams is differences of opinion. Two heads are better than one because they see things differently. Of course, different points of view will occasionally lead to conflict. Organizational members need tools to deal with conflict when it arises. I will discuss the tools or interventions for managing conflict in Part II of this book.

Questionnaires will reveal the types and levels of conflict. Interviews may explain the roots or nature of various conflicts in the organization. Observations of meetings and person-to-person interactions indicate how conflict is handled.

Company documents may be less helpful here because they rarely explain the cultural expectations for conflict resolution. Employee performance evaluations may reveal who might need training in conflict management. Psychological instruments may also reveal individuals who are likely to be unyielding in conflict.

Anonymous letter writing provides insight into where negative conflict exists in the organization. Negative conflict may be limited to two particular individuals, or it may characterize the organization's culture.

Information sought concerning conflict includes:

1. What types of conflict exist?
2. Is positive conflict encouraged or stifled?
3. What are the norms for resolving conflict?
4. Which conflict management tools are currently used?
5. Does the reward system promote cooperation or conflict?

Organizational Learning

The process of organizational learning is perhaps the most misunderstood of the target processes. To maintain a competitive advantage, organizations must encourage, provide, capture, and utilize the on-going learning of organizational members. For profit-seeking organizations, especially those in high-tech or highly competitive industries, the organizational learning process of the company can make or break the firm. I will devote Chapter 12 of this book to organizational learning systems and interventions.

Questionnaires reveal the types of learning that are encouraged in the organization. Interviews disclose how the organization supports and rewards on-going learning. Observations of new employee orientation sessions show whether a learning organization culture exists or not.

Company documents, such as budgets and intranet postings, indicate the level of commitment senior management has to employee learning and development. Employee performance evaluations should discuss learning needs and learning plans.

Psychological instruments indicate the individual learning preferences of organizational members. I will discuss this further in the chapter on organizational learning.

Anonymous letter writing reveals much about the organizational culture in general and about the pervasiveness of organizational learning in particular.

Information sought about organizational learning includes:

1. Is learning occurring at all levels of the organization?
2. How is new learning "captured"?
3. Are learning needs discussed as part of performance evaluations?
4. Do employees make learning and development agreements?
5. How is new learning rewarded?

Summary

No doubt some OC researchers and practitioners will consider my data-gathering model too simplistic, but please receive it in the spirit in which it is offered. My model is a practice guide. Practitioners should add to or delete from it as they see fit.

I believe using the six data-gathering methods for six target groups and six target processes will get the OC consultant through most client situations. Once the data is gathered, then what? That's the topic of the next chapter.

CHAPTER 6

Feedback, Diagnosis, and Action Planning

The second, third, and fourth steps in the Action Research Model are feedback, diagnosis, and action planning. A dramatic difference between the Action Research Model (and the Process Consultation Model) and the traditional Expert Model is the collaborative work on feedback, diagnosis, and action planning. The traditional Expert Model simply provides for the consultant's gathering data, and then offering a diagnosis and action plan (the client has little or no input).

The Feedback Step

In the Action Research Model and in Schein's Process Consultation Model, the client is actively involved throughout the OC engagement. Feeding back the recently gathered data to the client and working on a joint diagnosis with the client serve two important purposes:

1. The consultant can confirm his/her perceptions of the data.
2. The client's critical input remains available throughout the process.

For the feedback step to be successful, the OC consultant must be concerned with both the content (the "what") and the process (the "how") of feedback. As the previous chapter indicates, large amounts of organizational data can be gathered during Action Research step 1. Simply dumping large piles of data on clients is not helpful. That will discourage the client, perhaps to the point of giving up on the change effort.

Content (the "What") of Feedback

Determining the content of the feedback is the responsibility of the OC consultant. The consultant must summarize and categorize what could be an overwhelming amount of data for the client to interpret.

I can offer a few suggestions here. The data should be meaningful and significant to the client members. An understanding of the organization's culture is necessary to determine meaning and significance. Comparing the organization's data to industry averages, or to that of competitors, can add perspective to the data.

Perhaps most importantly, the data being fed back must be understandable. Pie charts and tables for quantitative data and specific examples for qualitative data can enhance problem identification. If the problem(s) is/are not understood or recognized, it is unlikely the client members will devote energy to solving it/them.

Process (the "How") of Feedback

The OC consultant must send a very clear message during the feedback session — the data is not in final form. The consultant should state that the data is being presented to stimulate an in-depth discussion about the target groups and target processes.

The OC consultant should be prepared to deal with some fear and defensive behaviors. Remember, this is a new experience for most of the client members.

I recommend meeting with group leaders before the feedback meeting to alert them to potentially explosive issues. Group and departmental leaders do not appreciate unpleasant surprises in these feedback sessions. If change efforts are to succeed, it is critical to garner the support of organizational leaders.

While feedback meetings should be open to comments from every attendee, the meeting should have some structure. An agenda will legitimize the consultant's occasional requests to move on from unproductive discussions. A meeting that is derailed by chaos and name calling can establish a resistant tone that persists throughout the engagement.

A general rule for who should attend is: if an individual is part of the problem, or part of the solution he or she should attend the feedback session.

The success of the feedback session depends on the skills of the OC consultant. Group process skills are necessary to keep the group in a problem-solving mode. The feedback session itself can be a powerful team-building intervention if properly facilitated by the consultant.

Speed is not the goal of the feedback meeting. In fact, the consultant may want to suggest a separate (later) meeting for diagnosis, if the discussion of the feedback data is especially productive. I usually arrive at these meetings with a *pencil copy* of the themes I have gathered; I do not want to indicate that I have reached any conclusions.

Survey Feedback Method

One feedback model that has historical significance is the Survey Feedback Method. Originally, the Survey Feedback Method was used to collect data about member attitudes. Some early advocates of the Method attributed "large across-the-board positive changes in organizational climate" to its use (Bowers, 1973). Later researchers (Friedlander and Brown, 1974; Pasmore, 1976) questioned whether the Survey Feedback Method alone could result in significant individual or organizational changes. I believe the Survey Feedback Method is an effective diagnostic tool, but it must be used with appropriate interventions (discussed in Part II of this book) to affect significant organizational change.

The steps of the Survey Feedback Method, while modified by each practitioner, go roughly as follows:

1. Consultant and client members agree on objectives for data gathering and diagnosis.

2. A survey instrument is developed or a standardized questionnaire is chosen.

3. The instrument is administered to a large number of client members (larger numbers encourage greater buy-in).

4. Consultant tabulates the results.

5. Consultant trains client members to lead feedback sessions.

6. Feedback sessions begin with top management (consultant acts as facilitator).

7. Feedback sessions occur at successively lower levels in the organization (a cascading or waterfall approach).

The multiple feedback sessions in a top-down approach (some practitioners use a bottom-up approach) follow this format:

1. The group addresses problems/issues under its control, and develops action plans.

2. The group makes suggestions for problems/issues beyond its control.

3. Combined data is fed down (or possibly up) to the next level of management.

4. Management reviews previous group's action plan and considers suggestions offered.

While there are a number of variations, practitioners believe the less directive role of the facilitator allows the organizational members themselves to learn the process.

The Survey Feedback Method is inappropriate in some situations. Where there are high levels of distrust or "unmentionable" topics, the model will be ineffective. Also, the initial step of determining the objectives and choosing a survey instrument requires consensus. In some organizations reaching this consensus may be extremely difficult.

The Diagnosis Step

Once the data gathering and feedback steps are completed, the massive amounts of data must be analyzed. This diagnostic step, when done well, should make the selection of appropriate interventions rather easy.

The diagnostic step of the Action Research Model (and Schein's Process Consultation Model) is different from the diagnostic step in the traditional Expert Model (or Doctor-Patient Model) in two substantial ways:

1. The Action Research Model (and the PC Model) sees the diagnostic step as collaborative — consultant and client working together as equals.

2. The Doctor-Patient Model assumes that something is wrong; the

Action Research Model (and PC model) assumes there are opportunities as well as problems.

There are two related concepts to keep in mind when doing diagnostic work: systems theory and open-systems theory. Systems thinking, based on systems theory, keeps OC consultants from falling into the trap of looking for problem people. Rarely is an organizational problem so simplistic that it can be solved by removing and replacing a single employee. Most organizational problems are systemic. Unless the system is changed, the replacement employees will have to deal with the same problems.

The OC consultant must also remember that every system (entire organization, large subsystem, group/team, dyad, or individual) is "open," which means it must interact with the larger environment of which it is a part. The individual is open to the group, in that he/she must interact with the group. Groups must be open or interactive with other parts of the organization. And, the organization itself must be open or interactive with its larger environment (customers, suppliers, lending institutions, and other stakeholders).

One other concept must remain in focus as the OC consultant does diagnostic work with the client. Diagnosis is basically the search for "misfits" in the organization. Organizational fit or alignment must be established (and maintained) between the organization's strategy, structure, culture, and processes. Fit must also exist at different levels: the individual job or member must fit the group, groups must fit the organization, and the organization must fit its environment.

Let's look at diagnosis at the three different levels: the organizational level, the group level, and the individual job or member level.

Organizational-Level Diagnosis

At the organizational level it is critical that a well-crafted strategic plan be in place. All the other functions and processes of the organization must fit this strategic plan. Interventions for a weak or non-existent strategic plan will be covered in Chapter 7.

The organization's structure, culture, and human processes must be designed to support the strategy. Aligning all four of these aspects of the organization is one of the primary responsibilities of senior management. No organization will succeed in today's competitive environment unless these four aspects are aligned. The importance of organizational fit cannot be overstated.

Diagnosing the company's structure involves analyzing how effectively it is organized to accomplish its strategic plan. Structure involves the distribution of work and the authority to make decisions about how the work gets done. Work must be distributed to units or departments with the appropriate expertise. Jobs within those units must be designed to effectively use resources (human, financial, and physical assets). The utilization of technology in each of these areas should be analyzed. Finally, the coordination of the various organization's units should be reviewed. Competitive advantage can be created through the development of highly effective technostructural design. We will discuss structural interventions in Chapter 8.

Organizational culture has received much attention in management literature over the past few years. Culture develops over long periods of time. Culture — the shared norms, values, and assumptions — of the organization is usually deeply rooted and taken for granted. The diagnosis of culture begins with observing behaviors. Then the OC consultant must dig deeper to uncover the norms, values, and assumptions that drive those behaviors. Organizational cultural change can be very difficult because it often requires changing the basic assumptions that created the organization's norms and values. We will discuss organizational culture change interventions, both direct and indirect, in Chapter 9.

At the organizational level, the OC consultant must also consider an organization's human processes — how things get done, such as:

1. how teams are determined
2. how decisions are made
3. how information is disseminated
4. how employees are compensated

5. how conflict is handled
6. how success is measured

Many organizational problems can be traced to poorly designed or maintained human processes (how things get done). We will cover human process interventions in Chapters 10 through 12.

Most organizations generate a large number of reports. These reports, sometimes voluminous, should not be ignored by the OC consultant. Reports on financial results (profit/losses, sales trends, cost trends, quality) and stakeholder satisfaction (customers, employees, investors) can be very enlightening.

Keep in mind, we are looking for fit (i.e., alignment) of the organization's strategy, structure, culture, and human processes.

Group-Level Diagnosis

Diagnosing groups should take place after organizational diagnosis because the organization is the environment in which the group must operate. The group is imbedded in the strategy, structure, culture, and human processes of the organization.

A large group, or subsystem, can be analyzed much the same way as an entire organization. In a small group, or face-to-face team, analysis needs to focus on group dynamics and interpersonal interaction patterns.

Groups should receive periodic performance evaluations, including evaluations by superiors, subordinates, and peer groups (much like the periodic performance evaluations for individual employees). Unfortunately, many companies do not regularly evaluate teams.

Fortunately, models for diagnosing work groups do exist (Hackman and Morris, 1975; McCaskey, 1997). Basically, five questions must be considered when diagnosing the group:

1. Does the group have a clear purpose with measurable goals?
2. Is the work design of the group effective?
3. Does the group have the combined KSAs to accomplish its task?

4. Are disagreements/conflicts handled effectively?

5. Does the group receive feedback on its performance?

Groups should be assessed on two dimensions: task performance and quality of worklife. These two dimensions are essentially the same two Blake and Mouton use to assess leaders.

Group design should fit organizational design and allow for effective alignment of functioning with other groups. While varying in degree from company to company, each group should have the necessary autonomy and authority to assign tasks to members, to decide on production methods, and to set performance standards.

Many of the interventions discussed in Part II of this book are very effective for groups and teams, as well as for entire organizations. OC practitioners typically spend much time working at the group/team level of the organization.

Individual-Level Diagnosis

Diagnosis at this level looks at individual jobs and/or individual organizational members. Strategy, structure, culture, and human processes at this level are deeply imbedded in those of the group and in those of the overall organization.

When analyzing individual jobs, Hackman and Oldham's model is invaluable. Hackman and Oldham (1980) believe job design has five key dimensions:

1. skill variety — the range of skills utilized

2. task identity — identifiable accomplishment

3. task significance — the impact on others

4. autonomy — freedom and discretion

5. feedback — results and effectiveness are known

Analyzing these job dimensions can provide insight into how to make a job more intrinsically motivating. It is assumed the employee will be more productive if the job becomes more motivating.

Once again, fit is important at this level. An individual job design must promote the successful performance of the group. An individual member who is able to contribute effectively to the group will feel like a valuable member of the team.

A considerable amount of information about the individual member is probably already available through performance evaluations and HR documents. What might be lacking is an analysis of the fit of the employee's goals with the organization's goals. Reviewing the psychological instruments completed by the individual member will provide insight here. We will cover interventions for individual managers in Chapter 11.

Diagnostic Techniques

There are two broad categories of diagnostic tools: qualitative and quantitative. Choosing between qualitative and quantitative techniques is determined by the type of data that has been gathered. Qualitative techniques are useful in analyzing the deeper, richer data of interviews. Quantitative methods are useful in "crunching" (compiling and analyzing) the large numbers of responses to questionnaires.

For real-world purposes, the OC consultant should also consider the type of client he or she is working with. Some of my clients are very impressed by number-crunching (i.e., statistical information), so I provide them with as much quantitative analysis as possible.

Two popular qualitative methods are Forcefield Analysis and Content Analysis. Lewin's Forcefield Analysis, which was introduced earlier, views every organization's situation as a status quo resulting from driving forces and resisting forces pushing against each other. The task of the OC consultant is to determine who or what makes up the driving and resisting forces. Remember, the status quo benefits somebody, and he or she will defend against any perceived losses. Forcefield Analysis is an effective practice tool because the client can visualize the situation if the consultant draws a picture of the forces pushing against each other.

Content Analysis is frequently the diagnostic tool of choice when researchers work with interview data. Content Analysis attempts to categorize numerous, disparate interview comments into common themes. Weber's (1990) *Basic Content Analysis* describes the process. Basically, content analysis has three steps:

1. Responses are read to determine the range of responses.
2. Recurring responses, or themes, are used to establish categories.
3. All respondent answers are placed into appropriate categories.

Quantitative techniques, aided by statistical computer software, can be used to produce frequency distributions, scattergrams, and sophisticated statistical analyses. These techniques can be very convincing because they can be visual (e.g., scattergrams) or can be supported by large numbers (e.g., statistical reports).

Computing averages (means) and standard deviations may not answer "why," but the sheer number of responses can get the attention of organizational leaders. For example, if the mean response for 800 employees on a job satisfaction survey is less than two (on a scale of one to five), management members cannot deny there is a problem.

Frequency distributions go beyond mean scores to present different patterns of responses. Occasionally, extreme responses get lost in averages (means) because the extremes balance out. Frequency distributions provide insight into extremes and various patterns of perceptions in an organization.

One technique I have found to be especially effective in working with clients is the scattergram. Scattergrams provide a visual for relationships. Relationships between two variables can be positive, negative, or non-existent. In the figures below the relationships between the variables are clear.

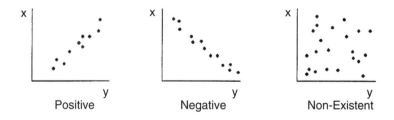

| Positive | Negative | Non-Existent |

The Action Planning Step

When most people think of an OC practitioner, they picture a consultant with a "bag of tricks." What has been referred to as the tricks of the profession are actually a wide selection of interventions (planned activities). What may appear to the untrained eye as a magician pulling magical solutions from a bag of tricks is, in fact, not magic at all. What the OC consultant can offer his or her client is a host of proven techniques — interventions — to deal with organizational problems.

The trick is for the OC consultant to choose the appropriate intervention(s). Prerequisites for making an appropriate choice include establishing an effective consultant-client relationship, data gathering, feedback, and diagnosis (the topics of chapters one through six). Choosing an *inappropriate* intervention(s) will surely lead to disappointment.

What Is an Intervention?

Many of my students and clients have heard about OC interventions. They have heard about restructuring entire corporate divisions, changing organizational cultures from autocratic to participative, and resolving intergroup conflict.

Understandably, they want to start with interventions (step four in the Action Research Model), simply jumping over the hard work of data gathering, feedback, and diagnosis (the first three steps in Action Research). It is important to realize that the interventions, in that "bag of tricks," don't hold any magical powers in themselves. Unless the intervention is based on a thorough diagnosis, it will not lead to positive change.

What is an intervention? An intervention is a set of planned activities with the goal of changing a collaboratively diagnosed problem.

"How many interventions are there?" asked my student with test anxiety. When I told him that there isn't a fixed number, he put down his pencil with some obvious frustration. His question indicates a commonly held misunderstanding about interventions. OC interventions are simply planned activities that are tailored to resolve the organization's diagnosed problem. Since no two organizational problems are identical, no two intervention efforts should be identical.

There are numerous interventions that are tried and proven (we will look at many of them in chapters seven through twelve). Some of these interventions have been used for many years with great success. Some have their own names and related success stories. Some interventions have been given credit for changes of Biblical proportions (some have loud advocates).

Generally speaking, it is not wise to simply pull an intervention from the OC consultant's "bag of tricks" and apply it without a thorough diagnosis. Some tailoring of each intervention, as presented later in this book, is necessary.

How to Tailor the Intervention

Since every intervention must be tailored to the unique problem that has been diagnosed in a particular organization, some guidance in tailoring is helpful. French and Bell (1999, pp.146-47) offer nine suggestions for structuring (i.e., designing) the intervention:

1. Include all of the relevant people (the people affected by the problem or the opportunity).

2. Focus on problems or opportunities that have the highest priority for the client. These activities will have the greatest support.

3. Be sure the goal of the intervention is clear. Organizational members need to know how what they are doing contributes to goal attainment.

4. Goals should be challenging but attainable. Practitioners' and clients' expectations should be realistic.

5. Use both experience-based learning and conceptual learning. Experience becomes a permanent part of the individual's knowledge base when put into a conceptual/theoretical frame.

6. Create a climate where individuals are "freed-up" rather than anxious or defensive. The climate should promote learning together in an experimenting way.

7. Help participants to solve a particular problem and to learn the

Session #18 & #19
★Q3 important
For Exam
Article in Email
& Know the traps
and Solutions.

process of effective problem solving. The client members can use the problem-solving skills learned in this intervention for future problems as well.

8. Participants should learn about human processes, including group processes and individual styles of interacting.

9. Allow for the discussion and expression of thoughts, feelings, and beliefs.

Using Multiple Interventions

Two decades ago, Michael Beer (1980) gave OC consultants some advice about how to integrate multiple interventions efficiently and effectively. Let me summarize his comments here.

1. Use data from early interventions to modify the data gathered during the diagnostic process. Data gathering should be an on-going process. Maximize diagnostic data.

2. Sequence interventions so that early interventions enhance the effectiveness of subsequent interventions. Skills and attitudes learned in early interventions can be used during the remainder of, and after, the engagement.

3. Sequence interventions (activities) to conserve organizational resources of time, energy, and money. Wasting or duplicating effort at the client's expense will quickly lead to client resistance.

4. Sequence interventions to maximize relevance. Work with the client's top priorities first. (This is similar to French and Bell's second point, which was discussed earlier.)

Expected Results of OC Interventions

As I said earlier, some OC interventions have claimed results that are now part of OC tradition, heritage, and mythology. All OC interventions do **not** produce mythological results, but most, when appropriately applied, yield valuable benefits. French and Bell (1999) list the following possible benefits:

1. **Feedback** about individual and group effectiveness, expectations, and perceptions.

2. **Awareness** of dysfunctional norms, attitudes, and values.

3. **Increased interaction and communication** between individuals and groups. Research indicates that increased interaction increases "positive sentiments" and feelings toward others.

4. **Confrontation** leading to the "surfacing and examining of differences in beliefs, feelings, attitudes, values, or norms."

5. **New learning** about "social relationships, organizational dynamics and processes, and processes for managing change."

6. **Greater participation** in "problem solving, goal setting, and generating new ideas."

7. **Increased accountability** through clarifying people's responsibilities and role expectations.

8. **Increased energy and optimism** resulting from "visions of new possibilities."

The OC consultant should attempt to design as many of these benefits as possible into each intervention.

Types of OC Interventions

There are basically six types of OC interventions:

1. Strategic Planning Interventions

2. Structural Interventions

3. Cultural Change Interventions

4. Human Process Interventions

5. Management Development Interventions

6. Organizational Learning Interventions

The last three types of interventions are human process interventions.

Part II of this book will cover all six types of interventions (one chapter devoted to each type). Strategic planning interventions will be discussed in Chapter 7. Structural interventions will be covered in Chapter 8. Cultural change interventions will be reviewed in Chapter 9.

Human process interventions will be discussed in Chapters 10 through 12. Chapter 10 will focus on team-building and conflict-management interventions. Chapter 11 will be reserved for interventions available for improving the performance of individual managers. Chapter 12 will be devoted to the interventions that have been developed to enhance organizational learning.

Summary

It is essential that client members be actively involved in the feedback, diagnosis, and action planning steps. Client involvement is critical for the interventions chosen to be effective. Choosing the appropriate OC intervention is relatively easy after a carefully executed diagnosis.

REFERENCES

Beer, M. (1980). *Organization change and development.* Santa Monica, CA: Goodyear Publishing.

Bowers, D. (1973). OD techniques and their results in 23 organizations: The Michigan ICL study. *Journal of Applied Behavioral Science* (January-March), pp.21-43.

French, W. L. & Bell, C . H., Jr. (1999). *Organization development: Behavioral science interventions for organization improvement* (6th ed.). Upper Saddle River, NJ: Prentice-Hall.

Friedlander, F. & Brown, L. (1974). Organization development. In M. Rosenzweig & L. Porter (Eds.), *Annual Review of Psychology.* Palo Alto, CA: Annual Review.

Hackman, J. & Morris, C. (1975). Group tasks, group interaction process, and group performance effectiveness: A review and proposed integration. In L. Berkowitz (Ed.), *Advances in Experimental Social Psychology*, Vol. 9. New York: Academic Press.

Hackman, J. & Oldham, G. (1980). *Work redesign.* Reading, MA: Addison-Wesley.

McCaskey, M. (1997). Framework for analyzing work groups. *Harvard Business School Case 9-480-009.* Boston: Harvard Business School.

Pasmore, W. (1976). Backfeed, the Michigan ICL study revisited: An alternative explanation of the results. *Journal of Applied Behavioral Science* (April-June), pp.245-51.

Weber, W. (1990). *Basic content analysis.* Thousand Oaks, CA: Sage Publishing.

CHAPTER 7

Strategic Planning Interventions

The most important target for change is the strategic plan at the organizational level. The strategic plan at the organizational level should affect everything that happens in the organization. Attempting to change the organization's structure, culture, or human processes without aligning them to a well-crafted strategic plan will be frustrating (and, ultimately, fruitless).

I strongly agree with Paul Buller (1988), who has recommended a blending of OC practices with strategic management. A strategy-driven approach to OC should be adopted by all practitioners.

PRACTICE LOG 7.1 — What's the Plan?
Late one morning my office phone rang, just as I was going out the door for an early lunch date. I hesitated. Then I thought, "I better answer that."

The gentleman on the other end of the line said, "Dr. Beitler, I understand that you do team building work for your clients."

"Yes," I responded and proceeded to tell him about some of the team building work I had done for other clients. (How I used different interventions in different situations.)

"Great!" he said with a sigh of relief. "Can you start right away?" he continued, "Our teams are out of control. They spend more time arguing and disagreeing over what needs to be done than they do actually working."

Realizing he was quite serious, I walked back around my desk and sat down. I decided to do some preliminary data gathering. I knew a little bit about the company. It was a profitable local organization with a fine reputation. I had assumed it was profitable and well managed.

My potential client went on to tell me about what was going on in the industry, how his company was losing market share to the competition, and how costs of production were rising dramatically.

While I found his comments to be interesting and informative, I was a bit confused about his original concern over teams. I interrupted by asking, "So, why did you switch to teams?"

Without hesitation, he said, "That's what the Japanese do," as if that should be obvious.

Since I found his "Japanese do it" argument for an American company's switching to a teamwork structure unconvincing, I suggested a meeting with his company's senior managers for some further analysis. We agreed on a date.

Then, I asked him to send me the organization's strategic plan and a few other company documents so that I could prepare for the meeting. He hesitated for a moment and said, "We don't have a **written** strategic plan. You probably don't understand that things change rapidly in our industry." Then with a snicker, he added, "A strategic plan would only apply for a few days around here."

I was beginning to see the problem, or at least a problem. The company was a ship without a rudder! We ended the phone call, and I ran out the door. (Incidentally, my lunch date forgave me for being late.)

Roles of Senior Management & the OC Consultant

Senior management must take the responsibility for a well-crafted strategic plan. While I am supportive of the new innovative ways of increasing employee involvement in the strategic planning process, the ultimate responsibility clearly belongs to senior management! There is no substitute for this leadership responsibility.

The role of the OC consultant in this process is that of facilitator. The OC consultant helps the company to strategically position itself in its competitive environment. This process requires an external analysis of the environmental opportunities and threats, as well as an internal analysis of the company's strengths and weaknesses. I believe the OC consultant should have some basic business knowledge (not necessarily an MBA) to work effectively in this area.

Looking for "Misfits"

Human resource (HR) professionals talk about the importance of "fit"; typically referring to "fitting" the person to the job. It's a basic concept, but very important. If the KSAs (knowledge, skills, and attitudes) of the worker/manager do not fit the KSAs of the job, effectiveness will suffer.

This concept of fit is also crucial in the organization's strategic planning process. The individuals must fit the team/group. The team/group must fit the larger subsystem. The subsystem must fit the organization. The organization itself must fit its larger environment.

At the entire organization level, senior management is responsible for analyzing the organization's fit with its environment. Subsequent strategic plans and goals set by managers at lower levels must fit their larger subsystem. Clearly, managers at lower levels of the organization cannot effectively do strategic planning and goal setting until senior management fulfills its responsibility at the entire organizational level.

Getting Started — The Mission Statement

Every organization needs a mission statement. The mission statement defines who we are, what we do, and who our customers are. Every member of the organization needs to know the purpose of the organization. The mission statement provides a shared vision for the members.

Once the mission statement is clear, a strategic plan must be crafted to fulfill the organization's mission. I will share several interventions in this chapter that OC consultants can use to facilitate this process.

Strategic Planning — SWOT Analysis

An organization is an open system. (We discussed open systems in Chapter 2.) While an organization (or system) is made up of many subsystems, it is important to remember that the organization (or system) is dependent upon its larger, external environment. An organization's environment includes its customers, suppliers, stockholders (owners), competitors, government regulators, the media, the community, and other stakeholders. The organization (system) is "open" in the sense that it is constantly interacting with, and influenced by, its environment.

These environmental influences require a thorough analysis. Most of the interventions shared in this chapter involve some form of a SWOT analysis. SWOT is an acronym for strengths, weaknesses, opportunities, and threats. The strategic plan must consider the strengths and weaknesses of the organization (internal analysis) and the opportunities and threats in the environment (external analysis).

Since the organization is dependent upon its environment for survival, it is essential to do the external analysis ("O" and "T") first; then conduct an internal analysis ("S" and "W") to plan a proper response to that environment.

Sustainable Competitive Advantage

The SWOT analysis must result in a clear, sustainable competitive advantage for the profit-oriented business organization. Even the not-for-profit charitable organization must serve a unique purpose in its environment, if it hopes to maintain a steady revenue stream.

The sustainable competitive advantage should leverage the organization's core competencies. Core competencies are what the organization can do better than the competition (better customer service, shorter delivery times, faster new product development, and higher quality, for example). The organization's unique core competencies should become the foundation of the strategic plan. The core competencies should be allocated the lion's share of resources for even greater development.

Organizational change consultants working as facilitators in the strategic planning process should familiarize themselves with the work of Michael Porter and others who address the issues involved in crafting and implementing an effective strategic plan (Porter, 1980, 1985).

Strategic Planning at Different Levels

The strategic planning/goal setting process should occur at every level of the organization. Each level (system) should have a strategic plan/goals that fit the strategic plan/goals of its larger subsystem. Every organizational unit (including individuals) should conduct a SWOT analysis.

Traditional Approaches to Strategic Planning

There are several traditional approaches, as well as some non-traditional approaches, currently being used as strategic planning interventions. Additionally, there are several ways of analyzing merger and acquisition (M&A) possibilities, and several transorganizational development (TD or TOD) interventions for analyzing joint ventures, strategic alliances, and other strategic possibilities. OC practitioners should be familiar with these approaches, methods, and tools. We will look first at some traditional approaches, then take a brief look at the non-traditional approaches, and conclude by reviewing the strategic planning process I have used in practice.

Charles Summer's Approach

Charles Summer's (1980) approach is simple but not quick. Summer's approach is based on four questions:

1. What is our present strategy?
2. What are our opportunities and threats?
3. What are our strengths and weaknesses?
4. What future strategies and/or tactics will avoid the threats and maximize our opportunities?

Summer believes senior management should ponder these four questions for up to a year, with monthly or bi-monthly meetings.

Thomas Rogers' Approach

Thomas Rogers' (1981) approach involves two-day meetings with senior management. Rogers begins with warm up questions that stimulate long-term thinking. Then the answer to the question, "What business are we in?" is worked into a mission statement.

Once the mission statement is agreed upon and clear, Rogers has the senior managers analyze the "domains" (stakeholders) who are influential in the organization's environment. The four domains or stakeholders, according to Rogers, are customers, suppliers, competitors, and regulators. The analysis of these domains or stakeholders involves the following steps:

1. Identify the various "domains" (stakeholders).
2. Identify the current demands of each.
3. Identify the current responses.
4. Predict future demands.
5. Identify desired future responses.

As the managers move back and forth between present and future, the need for change becomes a shared focus.

Beckhard and Harris' Approach

Beckhard and Harris (1987) offer a multi-step strategic planning process for organizations going through change. Senior managers are encouraged to consider multiple demands and multiple resources as they work through the following steps:

1. Determine the core mission of the organization.
2. Describe current demands.
3. Describe current responses.
4. Describe future demands with current responses.
5. Describe desired future.
6. Analyze discrepancies between #4 and #5.
7. Develop alternative responses.
8. Analyze feasibility, costs, and unintended consequences.

David Hanna's Approach

David Hanna's (1988) approach analyzes five key factors in the organization's performance (results). Hanna recommends an "outside-in" approach that begins with environmental scanning. He believes in developing an open organizational design that is responsive to the larger external environment.

Hanna's approach focuses on the following key variables:

1. business situation — the organization's current environment

2. business results — current outputs and profitability

3. business strategy — alignment of mission, goals, and values

4. design elements — structure, design, and information flow

5. organizational culture — supportive or counterproductive?

Hanna believes it is important to determine the organization's core tasks and processes in light of the demands and expectations of external stakeholders.

The Search Conference

The Search Conference has been a popular intervention in England, continental Europe, and Australia. Emery and Purser (1996) describe the Search Conference as a retreat-like, off-site event lasting for two and a half days.

The Search Conference involves three phases:

1. Environmental Appreciation — this looks at trends in the environment, as well as desirable and probable futures.

2. System Analysis — this examines the system's historical roots, current features, and its desirable future.

3. System Responses to Environment — this determines how to avoid threats and develops strategies and action plans.

Weisbord's Future Search Conference

The Future Search Conference, popular with American consultants, shares similarities with the European Search Conference. Weisbord (1987) describes this approach in his book, *Productive Workplaces*.

The OC consultant begins by conducting an initial meeting with four to six of the senior managers of the client organization. At this meeting, dates, location, and participant choices for a larger off-site meeting are determined.

At the off-site meeting location, the OC consultant must create the right climate. In this retreat-like setting, the casually dressed participants sit at round tables for six. Each table of participants (cross-functional group) is given an easel, flipchart, marking pens, and masking tape to record all ideas.

Each table of participants then follows these steps:

1. Analyze the internal and external forces
   External forces — reflected in current books and articles
   Internal forces — reflected in lists of "prouds" and "sorries"
2. Trace the roots of current trends
3. Draft a preferred future scenario
4. Report to the entire group
5. Discuss with entire group
6. Determine action steps in functional groups (as opposed to the earlier cross-functional groups)
7. Develop action plan with entire group

Beckhard's Confrontation Meeting

Richard Beckhard (1967) describes his Confrontation Meeting as a one-day meeting with the entire management. Beckhard believes his approach is appropriate when there is limited time, high levels of management commitment, and a need for major change.

The steps in the Confrontation Meeting are:

1. Climate setting by the top manager, who states goals of the meeting and invites open discussion. (Note: I recommend coaching from the OC consultant, before the meeting.)
2. Cross-functional groups gather responses from individuals about the needs, goals, obstacles of both individuals and the organization.
3. "Reporters" from each group report findings from each group on flipchart paper taped to the wall.
4. Reported items are categorized by the meeting leader into themes (e.g., communication, decision-making).
5. Functional groups prepare priority lists for senior management.
6. Everyone is dismissed except for the senior management team.
7. Top managers develop an action plan.

Non-Traditional Approaches

The newer, non-traditional approaches to strategic planning are more "open" to participation from members at all levels of the organization. Some of the steps in Beckhard's Confrontation Meeting are offensive to the advocates of the more "equalitarian" approaches to strategic planning. While I agree that inviting participation from many organizational members is beneficial for several reasons, don't forget the **ultimate responsibility** for the strategic plan is the job of senior management. The authority and responsibility in an organization must be allocated in equal measure.

Let's look at two of the newer, non-traditional strategic planning approaches: Real-Time Strategic Planning and the Open-Systems Meeting.

Real-Time Strategic Change

Robert Jacobs' (1994) Real Time Strategic Change approach is known as an "Open Systems Method" of strategic planning. Jacobs' approach involves a three-day event including all organizational members (or at least a critical mass). The three-day meeting has the following underlying assumptions:

1. The organization needs a new strategic direction based on internal and external drivers,
2. the leadership team has drafted a plan for consideration,
3. open feedback about the strategy is invited from all,
4. the proposed plan will be revised.

The large group (perhaps hundreds of participants) follows six steps:

1. Identify the major issues facing the organization.
2. Agree on overall purpose for the change.
3. Decide who needs to be involved in the change.
4. Determine what influence the people involved should have.
5. Clarify what information is needed to make decisions.
6. Provide support for people making decisions.

In Jacob's approach, most participation takes place in small groups known as "max-mix groups" (designed for maximum diversity of function and level). On the final day, participants self-select themselves on to action planning teams.

Organizational change consultants may have to work in teams themselves if they hope to successfully facilitate this large-group intervention. Jacobs (1994, p.247) reports on one 2,200-member event (at Ford's Dearborn, Michigan assembly plant) where thirteen OC consultants served as facilitators.

The Open Space Meeting

The Open Space approach is largely known for its lack of formal structure. Open-space methods restructure, at least temporarily, the entire organization. This temporary organization involves self-organized participants drawn together by topics or interests. Organizational members go wherever they like and participate in whatever topics they find interesting.

The first step in the Open Space Meeting is to create the conditions for self-organizing work groups. The OC consultant, or a well-coached manager, sets the stage by announcing the theme of the conference. Then he/she explains that small groups will convene to address any topic they deem as critical to the theme of the conference.

The facilitator describes the two distinctive sets of Open Space Meeting norms: The Law of Two Feet and The Four Principles.

The Law of Two Feet — you guessed it — allows participants to go to meetings and discussions where they are interested and or able to contribute. They can leave when they are no longer interested.

The second set of norms is known as the Four Principles:

1. Whoever attends are the right people.
2. Whenever it starts is the right time.
3. When it is over, it's over.
4. Whatever happens is the only outcome that could happen.

The second step in the Open Space Meeting involves creating the agenda. This step entails asking participants to describe a topic related to the conference theme that they are interested in discussing. The topic is written and placed on the community bulletin board to announce the topic, place, and time for discussion. Both sets of the Open Space Meeting norms apply to all of these meetings.

The final step involves collecting and disseminating the ideas and concerns from each meeting. The conveners of each meeting are responsible for producing a one-page meeting summary, and then posting it on a second bulletin board known as "the newsroom." Participants are encouraged to visit the newsroom often. (The newsroom's placement is typically near the refreshments and snacks.)

From this point, there are divergent approaches, including:

1. The strategic plan "crafters" are determined, or

2. the open-space meeting attendees develop strategic plans in groups, or

3. data from the sessions is turned over to senior management for strategic plan crafting (a more traditional approach).

While I appreciate the noble intentions (equalitarianism and full participation) of the non-traditional approaches, I believe these methods are costly, time-consuming, and generally ineffective.

Full participation is possible within the traditional approaches by simply including everybody in the data gathering phase (step one in the Action Research Model). Most employees understand that strategic planning is the responsibility of senior management. Typically, employees are satisfied with the opportunity to voice their opinions (in the data gathering phase), and to receive enough information about the plan to understand its purpose and rationale (clear communication from senior management). The non-traditional approaches appear to be an over-reaction to the closed-door, secret planning sessions of elitist management teams.

The Beitler Approach

The Beitler Approach to facilitating senior management strategic planning includes the steps I have found to be effective in my own practice.

1. Review the Current Mission Statement

Each member of the senior management team should share his/her vision for the organization. It is especially important for the CEO to share his/her vision last.

Once everybody has shared, an agreed-upon vision in the form of a mission statement should be written on flipchart paper and taped to the wall. This process can be quite time consuming, but it is extremely valuable for guiding subsequent discussions. The mission statement should clearly define the purpose (and customers) of the organization.

2. SWOT Analysis

This step, like step one, is very time consuming. A SWOT analysis is a lot of work. The OC consultant must work hard to keep everybody involved in an atmosphere of high energy and bold debate.

The first half of SWOT analysis is the OT (opportunities and threats). The discussion should begin with current threats and current responses, and then move to future threats with current responses. Future problems with current responses should be thoroughly discussed. Throughout the entire strategic planning process, input should be captured on flipchart paper and taped to the wall.

Once threats have been analyzed, it is time to discuss opportunities. The same pattern can be followed. Start with current opportunities and current responses, and then move to future opportunities with current responses. Any possible missed opportunities should be discussed.

Lastly, the external analysis (O and T) should include the identification of all external stakeholders and their stakes. Any threats? How should the company respond? Any opportunities? How should the company respond? External stakeholders include customers, suppliers, regulators, and other possible groups.

The second half of the SWOT analysis is the SW (strengths and weaknesses). The strengths and weaknesses of the organization should be discussed openly and honestly. Then the internal stakeholders and their stakes should be considered. Internal stakeholders include owner/ stockholders, employees, management, and other possible internal groups. The interests of internal stakeholders often conflict (e.g., large bonuses vs. large dividends).

3. Brainstorming Alternatives

Here the OC consultant must stimulate some right-brain creative thinking. The more alternatives the better. The goal is to maximize strengths and opportunities and to minimize weaknesses and threats. The consultant must be prepared to stimulate thinking "outside the box."

4. Feasibility and Consequences

It is important not to take a short cut here. This is not the place to save time. Each alternative strategy should be analyzed (left brain thinking) based on several criteria (cost, customer appeal, ease of implementation, and other considerations).

5. Choice of a Strategy

This is relatively easy if the first four steps are conducted properly.

6. Analysis of Organizational Support

Organizational support is essential for the successful implementation of a strategic plan. Do the current structure, culture, and processes offer support for the chosen strategy? If not, can the new strategy be implemented without changing other aspects of the organization?

7. Writing the Strategic Plan

The strategic plan itself should clearly describe how each functional area of the organization will contribute to the organization's success.

8. Development of Tactics

Tactics involve the steps that must be taken to execute the strategic plan. As in military operations, corporate strategy requires carefully planned tactical moves.

9. Assignment of Responsibility

In this step, the OC consultant should insist on assigning names to each responsibility. Everybody in the corporate world is so busy that he/she can only focus energy on what he/she is personally responsible for.

10. Communication and Follow-Up

The best crafted strategic plan will fail if it is not properly communicated. We can't follow a leader if we don't know where the leader is going. Finally, schedule follow-up meetings to check on progress. Discuss timetables; they are essential!

Frequently, discussion of one step makes the need to revisit an earlier step obvious. Encourage your client members to rethink those previous steps. Successful strategic planning is not characterized by speed. It is foolish to move fast when you are lost. Strategic planning involves determining the destination and best way to get there.

Mergers & Acquisitions (M&A)

Mergers and acquisitions (M&A) is a topic that should not be ignored by OC consultants. M&A is a growth strategy for many organizations. Responding to competitors (an external, environmental factor in the SWOT analysis) may call for an M&A strategy. Many companies have built empires using this strategy.

Mergers (the combination of equals) and acquisitions (the purchase of one company by another) produce enormous stress on the members of each organization. Galpin and Robinson (1997) have called M&As the "ultimate change management challenge."

M&A plans are frequently criticized as plans to make the rich richer. No doubt, some of those criticisms are true, but M&As do serve some legitimate purposes, including:

1. operational efficiencies
2. expanded product and service lines
3. access to global markets
4. shared R&D facilities

Despite their widespread use, numerous M&A deals have shown disappointing results. The reasons for M&A failure include paying too much, lack of due diligence, unrealistic expectations, conflicting corporate cultures, and poor strategic planning. Clearly, some of these reasons for failure can be avoided with the help of OC consultants.

M&A should involve three distinct phases: candidate analysis, legal/financial review, and post-transaction analysis. The candidate analysis phase should involve a variety of experts. OC consultants should be busy analyzing each organization's strategy, structure, culture, and processes. Other functional experts (financial, marketing, production, logistics, IT) should prepare reports on their areas of expertise.

The legal/financial phase must be handled by the lawyers, CPAs, and financial analysts who specialize in M&A. This is typically not an area of practice for most OC consultants.

The post-transaction phase is critical for M&A success. Ashkenas, DeMonaco, and Francis' (1998) work suggests making as many changes as possible in the first one hundred days after the completion of the deal. Clear and timely communication during this phase is also important to reduce uncertainty and anxiety for all stakeholders (stockholders, customers, employees, suppliers, and regulators).

Transorganizational Development (TD)

A final topic in strategic planning for OC consultants to consider is Transorganizational Development (TD). TD has become an important topic because of all of the possible intercompany relationships used to serve customers and to establish competitive advantage. These intercompany relationships include alliances, joint ventures, and licensing agreements, among others. These relationships are something less than mergers or acquisitions, but more than one-time transactions. These Transorganizational Systems (TSs) involve two or more independent companies working together for a common purpose. The TS may be temporary or permanent.

Transorganizational systems take a variety of forms. A TS may involve two competitors working together. One dramatic example was the joint venture between General Motors and Toyota to build cars together in Fremont, California. The TS had its own name (New United Motor Manufacturing, Inc.), its own strategy, its own structure, its own culture, and its own processes.

Other examples of TSs include research and development (R&D) consortia in various industries, such as semiconductors and pharmaceuticals. TSs frequently involve some form of vertical integration, such as agreements between manufacturers and suppliers, or between manufacturers and distributors.

International TSs are especially challenging because of differences in national culture, in addition to differences in organizational culture. But for practical purposes, it is nearly impossible for American and European companies to succeed in some markets (e.g., South American countries) without a local partner.

While TSs are not new, they still tend to be "underorganized." OC consultants may have to serve as advocates to develop the TS with the same principles and methods used in independent organizations. The TS needs leadership to provide vision, strategy, and structure, if the jointly owned organization is to succeed.

The role of the OC consultant in TD interventions is especially important. The OC consultant must possess well-developed political and networking skills to be effective.

Structure, Culture, Human Processes
Only after the OC consultant is convinced the company has a well-crafted, well-communicated strategic plan should he/she consider changes in the organization's structure, culture, or human processes.

REFERENCES

Ashkenas, R., DeMonaco, L., & Francis, S. (1998). Making the deal real: How GE Capital integrates acquisitions. *Harvard Business Review* (January-February).

Beckhard, R. (1967). The confrontation meeting. *Harvard Business Review*, 45 (March-April), pp.149-155.

Beckhard R. & Harris, R.T. (1987). *Organizational transitions: Managing complex change* (2nd ed.). Reading, MA: Addison-Wesley.

Buller, P. F. (1988). For successful strategic change: Blend OD practices with strategic management. *Organizational Dynamics*, 16, pp.42-55.

Emery, M. & Purser, R. E. (1996). *The search conference*. San Francisco: Jossey-Bass.

Galpin, T. & Robinson, D. (1997). Merger integration: The ultimate change management challenge. *Mergers and Acquisitions*, 31, pp.24-29.

Hanna, D. P. (1988). *Designing organizations for high performance*. Reading, MA: Addison-Wesley.

Jacobs, R. W. (1994). *Real time strategic change*. San Francisco: Berrett-Koehler.

Porter, M. (1980). *Competitive strategy*. New York: Free Press.

Porter, M. (1985). *Competitive advantage*. New York: Free Press.

Rogers, T. H. (1981). *Strategic planning: A major OD intervention*. ASTD Publications.

Summer, C. E. (1980). *Strategic behavior in business and government*. Boston: Little, Brown).

Weisbord, M.R. (1987). *Productive workplaces*. San Francisco: Jossey-Bass.

CHAPTER 8

Structural Interventions

Structural interventions, like strategic planning interventions, target different levels in the organization. We will look at structural interventions to enhance the effectiveness of individual jobs, group/ teams, and entire organizations. Let's start with the big picture — the entire organization.

I. The Entire Organization's Structure

Structuring the entire organization involves allocating responsibility and authority to the appropriate individuals or units in the organization. The goal of structural designing at this level is to support the company's strategic plan. An inappropriate organizational structure could make successful implementation of the strategic plan difficult, if not impossible.

When discussing structural design issues at any level of the organization, we have to return to the concept of "fit." The organizational structure must fit its environment, strategy, company size, and task (manufacturing, retailing, distributing). Additionally, the organizational structure must support and encourage the desired organizational culture (the subject of the next chapter).

Types of Organizational Structures

There are basically five possible structures at the entire organization level:

1. function-based
2. product/service-based
3. process-based
4. matrix-based
5. network-based

Function-Based Organizational Structures

The function-based organizational structure, the traditional structure, is arranged according to the functional areas of the particular organization: production, marketing, finance, IT, and HR. The function-based organizational structure typically looks like the following:

Figure 8.1 Function-Based Organizational Structures

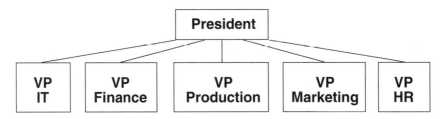

The function-based organizational structure has several advantages. Foremost, the structure promotes specialization and career development within that specialty. The functional area, typically a department, is headed by a specialist in the field. Individuals working in the department (function) have the career development opportunity of working with other specialists in their field.

The function-based structure also has some disadvantages. The most damaging disadvantage is the creation of a "silo-effect." With each department focused on its particular function, communication and cooperation between departments tend to decrease over time. Each department works within its silo, concerned only with its particular function. Cross-functional issues and accountability for overall outcomes tend to "fall through the cracks" between the departments.

The function-based structure is appropriate in certain situations. Companies operating in stable environments where the goal is the high speed production of an unchanging product could benefit from a function-based organizational structure.

Product/Service-Based Organizational Structures

Product/service-based organizational structures are organized around the particular company products, services, customers, or geography. Some form of product/service-based structure is used by all of the multinational conglomerates. Special-purpose subsystems can then specialize in a product, service, customer (e.g., government contracts), or a particular geographic area.

A product/service-based organization structure might look like the following figure:

Figure 8.2 Product/Service-Based Organizational Structures

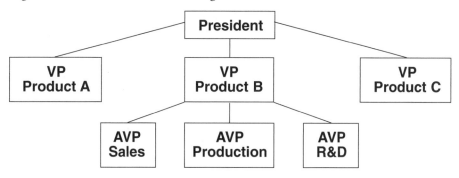

The advantages of the product/service-based organizational structure include cross-functional support for each product/ service line, and better overall accountability for success. This structure is particularly helpful for companies with diverse customers with widely differing needs.

The disadvantages of this structure include the duplication of some efforts, such as multiple sales teams (one for each product). This duplication can lead to inefficiencies in the use of knowledge, skills, and resources. This duplication can be disastrous in industries with low profit margins.

Process-Based Organizational Structures

Process-based organizational structures form cross-functional teams around company processes, such as customer support, new product development, or order processing. Process-based structures emphasize lateral relationships (Galbraith & Lawler, 1993). The process teams typically are supported by a few staff support departments (e.g., finance or HR). The other functions (e.g., purchasing) are handled by the process team.

The advantages of process-based structures include the elimination of several layers of hierarchy and the elimination of many functional boundaries. Several companies report success with these "boundaryless" organizations in enhancing customer service and satisfaction. Frequently, process teams are designed based on customer expectation surveys or market research.

Both the process-based and the product-based structures have the disadvantages of duplicating efforts and the inefficient consumption of scarce resources. Switching to process-based structures also requires a radical shift in thinking about managerial and worker roles and responsibility. Creating cultural support for process-based structures is time consuming, and difficult.

Matrix-Based Organizational Structures

Matrix-based organizational structures are attempts to combine the advantages of the functional structure (emphasizing the vertical) and the product/service structure (emphasizing the horizontal). Matrix structures are complex and sometimes confusing for workers. Workers in these structures have two bosses: one product/project supervisor and one functional supervisor. For example, an engineer may be reporting to a functional supervisor (VP for Engineering) and simultaneously be accountable to a project manager (Director of Project X for the State Government). Figure 8.3 on page 111 depicts a possible matrix structure:

There are multiple advantages for matrix structures. Foremost, this structure makes specialized, functional knowledge and skills available to all projects. Matrix structures also promote the flexible use of organizational talent. Organizational members expect to be uprooted and moved to other project teams on a regular basis.

Disadvantages include balancing power between functional and project supervisors. Unfortunately, unethical managers with well-developed political skills frequently take advantage of these structures. There is also the potential disadvantage of unclear role expectations. Unclear role expectations cause considerable anxiety for workers, ultimately reducing productivity.

While matrix organizational structures have several potential problems, they are becoming quite popular. Matrix structures are now used in manufacturing, service, and professional organizations. These structures can increase organizational effectiveness by allowing for the sharing of valuable organizational talent and resources.

Figure 8.3 Matrix-Based Organizational Structures

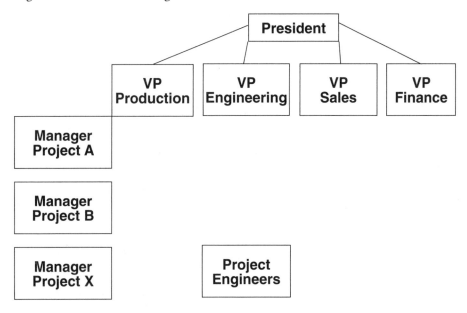

Network-Based Organizational Structures

The final form of organizational structure is the network-based structure. Chisolm (1998) describes four types of networks:

1. Internal Market Network — Within a single organization, independent profit centers buy and sell products and services to each other (internal customers), as well as to external customers.

2. Vertical Market Network — Multiple organizations work together to move products from raw materials to finished products, or sales, or through after-sales customer service. Each organization focuses on its own specialty.

3. Intermarket Network — Multiple organizations in different markets form an alliance to serve customers with widely varying needs.

4. Opportunity Networks — Temporary affiliations of organizations

with the purpose of taking advantage of a unique situation. Once the opportunity passes, the affiliation is dissolved.

Three of the four network structures (two, three, and four) described by Chisolm (1998) may be appropriate for implementing the transorganizational strategies discussed in Chapter 7. These network structures are frequently coordinated by "broker organizations" that play the role of general contractor (typically seen in the construction industry).

Network-based structures allow units or organizations to focus on what they do best. These structures often result in powerful synergies and rapid growth in market share.

There are, of course, some disadvantages to network structures. Independent organizations may be resistant to giving up their autonomy or proprietary knowledge. How to divide the benefits fairly may be difficult to agree upon.

I believe network-based structures will continue to grow because in many situations they are almost a requirement of success. Network-based structures allow for the efficient use of high-cost technologies and for global expansion.

Restructuring the Entire Organization

Sometimes it is necessary to change the organization's structure to fit the organization's strategy. A radical change in strategy typically demands a dramatic change in structure. Even if the organizational strategy is not changed, the organization's structure should be periodically examined to determine its effectiveness.

Organizational restructuring interventions vary in degree from minor adjustments to large-scale, organization-wide changes that affect virtually every organizational member. Large-scale radical redesign is commonly known as "re-engineering."

Re-engineering involves a fundamental rethinking of how the organization makes and delivers products and services. Questioning the shared assumptions underlying how the organization operates can be deeply disturbing for some organizational members, so the OC consultant must be highly trained in organizational change and group dynamics. Re-engineering the entire organization also requires restructuring at the group/team and individual job levels. Re-engineering is often associated with downsizing (our next topic) because radical restructuring to avoid duplications and inefficiencies typically results in fewer workers and/or fewer layers of management.

Cummings and Worley (2001, pp.304-306) believe cross-functional teams should follow these re-engineering steps:

1. Identify and analyze core business processes. (A company may improve efficiencies by outsourcing non-core processes.)

2. Define performance objectives. (These standards should be based on customer requirements, or on "benchmarks" and best practices of industry leaders.)

3. Design new processes to create a competitive advantage.

4. Restructure the organization around the new processes.

Cummings and Worley (2001) correctly add, "The business strategy should determine the focus of reengineering and guide decisions about the business processes" (p.303).

Downsizing

One type of restructuring that creates enormous angst throughout the organization is the dreaded "downsizing." Downsizing involves early retirements, redeployment, attrition, delayering, outsourcing, divestiture, and/or layoffs. Regardless of how the downsizing is accomplished, it always means one thing — fewer people. That outcome makes both terminated employees and survivors very uncomfortable.

The first people to go in corporate downsizings are the temporary and permanent part-time workers. Their work is outsourced to independent contractors or "spread around" to the permanent full-time employees. Outsourcing is potentially a wise way to restructure if another firm can do the task more efficiently. But the company should retain and continue refining its own core competencies.

Whether structuring or restructuring, the organization's structure should be clearly aligned with the organization's long-term strategy. OC consultants must be prepared to question senior management's attempts to obtain "quick fixes" at the expense of long-term plans. Downsizings, especially in the form of layoffs, can produce quick and dramatic short-term cost reductions, but can result in large (even if not clearly measurable) long-term opportunity costs.

In his best-selling textbook, *Psychology Applied to Work*, Paul Muchinsky discusses the impact of downsizing on the psychological contract (Muchinsky, 2000, pp.284-292). The psychological contract involves the unwritten expectations employees have concerning job security and promotion opportunities. Employees perceive a reciprocal agreement under which, hard work and loyalty to the company are rewarded with job security and promotion opportunities.

Muchinsky (2000) believes employees (both terminated and survivors) see downsizings and layoffs as a "fundamental violation" of the psychological contract. Violations of psychological contracts result in organizational cultures that are less relational and more transactional (Robinson, Kraatz, & Rousseau, 1994). Motivating surviving employees in the post-downsized environment is very difficult. "Downsizing emphasizes the cold and brutal reality that the goals of the individual and the goals of the organization need not necessarily align" (Muchinsky, 2000, p.289).

Surviving employees of downsizings will question the necessity of the downsizing, the criteria used for termination, and caretaking activities (severance pay and outplacement counseling, for example). OC consultants should be prepared to discuss these issues with the management team. The client should be aware of the possibility of good employees "jumping ship" and going to the competition.

II. Team/Group Structure

In recent years, we have seen a dramatic increase in the use of the team structure for accomplishing work in organizations. Some of the applications for the team structure have been appropriate and highly successful. On the other hand, some inappropriate uses of the team structure have produced poor results. The key for OC consultants and managers is to recognize when a team structure is appropriate and what type of team is called for.

Certain tasks, particularly those requiring some form of highly trained expertise, may be more appropriately handled by an individual expert. Inappropriate uses of teams are costly (both in terms of time and money) and frustrating for the team members. The OC consultant should devote time to analyzing the use of teams with client members.

There are basically three types of teams to consider:

1. **Creative teams** are called upon to explore possibilities and to present alternative ideas and solutions to management. Members of creative teams must be comfortable working "outside of the box." Brainstorming meetings of creative teams are unstructured, high-energy sessions that frequently produce "off-the-wall," non-traditional possibilities.

2. **Tactical teams** are responsible for executing a well-defined plan. The focus of these team members is on the execution of their highly focused, specific task. Team success is determined by meeting high pre-established performance standards. I know of one large bank that will "helicopter-in" a post-acquisition tactical team to examine the procedures of each new branch office. (A police SWAT team is another example.)

3. **Decision-making teams** are charged with the responsibility of gathering data, analyzing data, and coming to a decision. Members of decision-making teams must understand the impact and consequences of their decisions. The members of these teams need highly developed analytical and critical thinking skills.

To be successful, the HR knowledge applied to individuals must be applied to teams. Selection, compensation, evaluation, and training are also critical to team success.

Regarding selection, Muchinsky (2000) has stated, "traditional job analytic methods identifying the KSAs needed for individual job performance ... tend to be insensitive to the social context in which work occurs" (p.264). This is especially true when we are selecting members for teams. The team member selection process should consider learning styles, tolerance for stress, and risk-taking comfort levels.

Compensating and rewarding team members are also critical concerns. If team members continue to be rewarded for individual performance, they will not devote themselves to team success.

Periodic performance evaluation of the team is critical for on-going success. Human beings need feedback about their performance.

Training for teams, like training for individuals, involves helping members obtain the KSAs that are required by the job. Similar to individual training, a training needs analysis (TNA) for the team's task must be conducted first. Next, any deficient KSAs must be provided for.

Team development, like individual development, should be seen as an on-going process. I will devote a large part of Chapter 10 (Human Process Interventions) to team building interventions. There are several highly successful, proven interventions available for team building.

III. Individual Job Design

Muchinsky (2000, p.396) uses a "peg-and-hole" analogy to compare the HR functions of selection and training to job design. He sees "finding new pegs that fit existing holes" as the HR function of selecting, and "reshaping pegs for better fit" as the HR function of training. Muchinsky goes on to say that the problem of fit can also be approached by "changing the shape of the hole." Changing the shape of hole is the task of job design (or redesign). Muchinsky summarizes, "It is possible to change the workplace instead of, or in addition to, changing the worker" (p.396).

There are three different approaches to job design (job structure):

1. the engineering approach
2. the psychological approach
3. the sociotechnical approach

Engineering Approach to Job Design

The engineering approach to job design is rooted in the work of Frederick Taylor. Most business students know Taylor as the father of scientific management. The profession of industrial engineering is based on Taylor's principles for analyzing and designing work (Taylor, 1911).

The engineering approach seeks to maximize output (finished goods) and minimize input (energy and resources) by designing jobs with high levels of specialization and simplification. Taylor and his followers believed by simplifying a job, the job could be quickly learned and then executed with little or no mental effort.

In Taylor's time, this approach to job design made sense. The Industrial Revolution was under way, and large numbers of unskilled workers were moving to the big cities for work.

PRACTICE LOG 8.1 — It Pays the Bills!

When my ancestors emigrated from Germany, they were poor, uneducated, and didn't speak English. Realizing that they weren't executive material, they were willing (and thankful) to take any kind of work they could get. The goal was not self-actualization (in Maslow's terminology); the goal was to feed the family.

In Pennsylvania, the Beitlers had basically two careers to choose from: coal miner or farm hand. These were not exciting options, but they were typically the only options for the unskilled, uneducated immigrants.

Then a new option became available in the big cities — factory worker. Factory work in the big cities (Pittsburgh or Baltimore) provided a paycheck without digging in the topsoil (or digging hundreds of feet below the top soil). One visit to a coal mine will explain why my ancestors moved to Pittsburgh or Hagerstown (a smaller factory town in Western Maryland). My father dropped out of high school in Hagerstown to take a job working in an airplane manufacturing plant in Baltimore.

Unskilled, uneducated workers didn't complain about their routine, repetitive tasks. These jobs paid the bills. In the first half of the

1900s, factory workers expected strict schedules, rigid work flows, and autocratic bosses.

The engineering approach, with its focus on time-and-motion studies, came under severe criticism in the latter half of the 1900s. Critics charged that jobs designed with the engineering approach "dehumanized" the worker. Personally, I believe the critics fail to appreciate the significant contributions of the engineering approach.

When the engineering (technical) approach is combined with the psychological approach (discussed next) a highly effective sociotechnical approach emerges. Let's look at the psychological approach next, and then the sociotechnical approach.

Psychological Approach to Job Design

The psychological approach to job design became more popular as workers became better educated. By the latter half of the twentieth century, workers were no longer content with a paycheck alone.

Researchers following the psychological approach concluded that monotonous jobs were not as productive as previously predicted. Melamed, Ben-Avi, Luz, and Green (1995) spoke of "underload" producing a type of counterproductive stress. Underload is an insufficient amount (or lack of) of job stimulation. Wong and Campion (1991) suggested a medium range of stimulation to make jobs more satisfying.

In the latter half of the twentieth century, job designers began to use the terms "job enlargement" and "job enrichment." Job enlargement involves increasing the variety of tasks performed by a particular worker (a horizontal change). Job enrichment involves increasing a worker's control, authority, and responsibility over a particular job (a vertical change). Job enrichment advocates believe by satisfying a worker's higher needs (e.g., autonomy and decision-making power), jobs will become more motivating.

By the mid-1960s, researchers following the psychological approach were looking at task attributes that influenced worker behavior. Turner and Lawrence (1965) identified several attributes that lead to worker satisfaction and attendance: variety, autonomy, interaction (required and optional), required knowledge and skills, and responsibility. It became apparent that not all workers responded uniformly to the same task attributes. Muchinsky (2000) concludes, "people trying to satisfy higher-order needs want more stimulating jobs. They ... respond more positively to enriched jobs" (p.399).

Hackman and Oldham made two valuable contributions to OC practice in 1975 and 1976. They created the Higher-Order Need Strength Questionnaire B (Hackman & Oldham, 1975) to identify individuals who would respond positively to enriched jobs. Then they developed the Job Characteristics Model (Hackman & Oldham, 1976) to help job (re)designers determine the motivating potential of particular jobs based on five core job dimensions:

1. skill variety
2. task identity
3. task significance
4. autonomy
5. feedback

The first three characteristics (skill variety, task identity, and task significance) influence the perceived meaningfulness of the job. Simply put, skill variety involves the opportunity to use a variety of skills; task identity provides the sense of completing a "whole" task; and task significance represents a positive impact on others.

The fourth characteristic, autonomy, allows the worker to experience responsibility for outcomes. The final characteristic, feedback, provides the worker with knowledge about results and input for future growth.

Hackman and Oldham's (1975, 1976) contributions are essential additions to the OC consultant's tool kit. Redesigned jobs can create increased worker satisfaction and greater organizational productivity — a win/win situation!

Sociotechnical Approach to Job Design
The sociotechnical approach, also known as the sociotechnical systems

(STS) approach, is rooted in the work of Eric Trist at the Tavistock Institute in London. After World War II, the British government privatized the coal mining industry. Even though substantial investments were made in new technology (much of which was developed during WW II), coal mining production did not improve. Trist studied the situation, and concluded that technological gains were being offset by losses in productivity due to social and psychological consequences. Breaking up teams, isolating workers, and reducing task identity reduced worker satisfaction and productivity.

Trist and followers of the STS approach insist that jobs must be designed to optimize both social and technical aspects. The social aspects operate according to biological and psychological laws; the technical aspects function according to mechanical and physical laws (Cummings & Worley, 2001, p.353). "Sociotechnical" suggests an interaction between both aspects.

Much of what we know about team design in general, and self-managed teams in particular, has grown out of the STS approach to job and team design.

Summary

Structural interventions should be considered only after a well-crafted strategic plan is in place. The strategic plan for the entire organization should be the starting point for considering the appropriate structure for the organization. The strategic plan, or goals and objectives, should be the starting point for the group or team. And finally, the goals and objectives of a particular job should determine its design or structure. Strategy should always precede structure.

Organizational change consultants must be familiar with alternative structures for clients at the entire organization level, the group/team level, and the individual job level. While structural interventions should be planned and implemented collaboratively with the client, the OC consultant must be prepared to facilitate the process.

REFERENCES

Chisolm, R. (1998). *Developing network organizations: Learning from theory and practice.* Reading, MA: Addison-Wesley.

Cummings, T.G. & Worley, C.G. (2001). *Organization development and change* (7th ed). Cincinnati, OH: South-Western.

Galbraith, J. & Lawler, E. (1993). *Organizing for the future: The new logic for managing complex organizations.* San Francisco: Jossey-Bass.

Hackman, J.R. & Oldham, G.R. (1975). Development of the Job Diagnostic Survey. *Journal of Applied Psychology,* 60, 159-170.

Hackman, J.R. & Oldham, G.R. (1976). Motivation through the design of work: Test of a theory. *Organizational and Human Performance,* 16, 250-279.

Melamed, S., Ben-Avi, I., Luz, J., & Green, M. (1995). Objective and subjective work monitoring: Effects on job satisfaction, psychological distress, and absenteeism in blue-collar workers. *Journal of Applied Psychology,* 80, 29-42.

Muchinsky, P. M. (2000). *Psychology applied to work* (6th ed.).Belmont, CA: Wadsworth/ Thomson Learning.

Robinson, S.L., Kraatz, M.S., & Rousseau, D.M. (1994). Changing obligations and the psychological contract: A longitudinal study. *Academy of Management Journal,* 37, 137-152.

Taylor, F. W. (1911). *The principles of scientific management.* New York: Harper & Row.

Turner, A.N. & Lawrence, P.R. (1965). *Industrial jobs and the worker: An investigation of response to task attributes.* Cambridge, MA: Harvard University Press.

Trist, E., Higgin, B., Murray, H., & Pollock, A. (1963). *Organizational choice.* London: Tavistock.

Wong, C. & Campion, M.A. (1991). Development and test of a task level model of motivational job design. *Journal of Applied Psychology,* 76, 825-837.

CHAPTER 9

Organizational Culture Interventions

In Chapter 1, I shared my practice model showing Organizational Culture on the bottom.

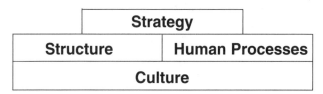

FIGURE 9.1

Let me explain. Organizational culture has some unique characteristics.

Indirect Changes

Organizational culture can be changed indirectly, as well as directly. When changes are made to the organization's strategy, structure, or human processes, changes (either positive or negative) will inevitably occur in the organizational culture. The other three elements (strategy, structure, and human processes) are embedded in the organizational culture.

Organizational culture will change if strategy is changed from low-cost leader to high-end niche provider. Changing to cross-functional teams, changing reward systems, and/or changing decision-making policies will lead to organizational culture change. Even though these changes are indirect, they can result in dramatic changes in the organization's culture — positive or negative. Senior management must consider these indirect culture changes when implementing changes in strategy, structure, and human processes.

Direct Changes

Much has been written about directly changing organizational culture. It's an exciting topic for executives and OC consultants because of the enormous potential benefits derived from changing an organization's culture. While exciting because of its **enormous potential**, attempting to directly change organizational culture can lead to **enormous frustration.**

It is important to understand how deeply the roots of organizational culture go. Organizational culture is rooted in the shared basic assumptions of the organization, which drive behavior throughout the organization. See Figure 9.2.

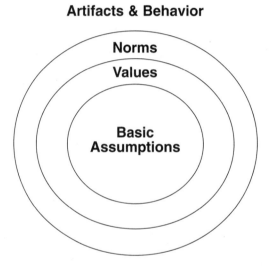

FIGURE 9.2

Edgar Schein, perhaps the most insightful author on organizational culture, shares several important insights about the nature of culture and human beings. Schein (1992) states, "culture implies some level of structural stability in the group" (p.10). He believes humans need stability, consistency, and meaning. Therefore, the creation of an organizational culture is "a striving towards stability, consistency, and meaning" (p.11).

After years of development, it is unlikely that organizational culture will change easily. The basic assumptions underlying the organization's behaviors, norms, and values cease to be questioned or debated.

Three German researchers (Schreyoegg, Oechsler, & Waechter, 1995) believe the basis of a culture is a fundamental orientation that shapes perceptions and actions. This world point of view "tells organizational members, in a subconscious way, how to perceive, how to conceptualize, and how to make decisions" (p.171).

Different Approaches to Studying the Phenomenon

There are dramatically different approaches to studying organizational culture (e.g., anthropological versus clinical). These different approaches result in very different understandings of the phenomenon we call organizational culture.

Despite these differences, Schreyoegg, Oechsler, and Waechter's (1995, pp.169-70)) review of the literature revealed the following core elements:

1. An Implicit Phenomenon

2. Everyday Practice

3. Shared — resulting in uniform thinking and acting

4. Historically Rooted — resulting from how problem situations with external challenges and internal integration was dealt with in the past

5. Guidelines for "Sense Making" — provides individual members with orientation schemes or ways to conceptualize complex situations

6. A Socialization Process — new members are taught the culture's expectations and traditions

My Simplistic Definition

For our purposes, let's use the following simplistic definition of organizational culture:

> *The shared basic assumptions an organization teaches its new members about the correct way to behave, think, and evaluate.*

Levels of Organizational Culture

While Schein (1992) and I disagree on the number of levels of organizational culture (Schein sees three; I see four), we agree that an understanding of an organization's culture must involve an analysis of the specific organization's values and basic assumptions. Simply evaluating or judging the observable artifacts and behaviors will not lead to cultural understanding. The deepest levels must be examined before observable artifacts and behaviors can be understood in context.

What we see when we walk into an organization are its **artifacts** (furniture, art work, posters) and "normal" **behavior** (normal by the organization's standards). There are frequently conflicting messages at the surface level. It is not uncommon for me to read banners on the wall proclaiming "Teamwork Makes Us Great!" or "The Customer is Number 1!", while observing employees working in individual cubicles, apparently oblivious to the existence of fellow employees or customers.

Just below the surface level, the observables, are **norms**. These accepted organizational norms drive the behavior of the organizational members. Norms gain legitimacy and power when organizational members reward and punish according to adherence to the norms. Let me offer the following example:

PRACTICE LOG 9.1 "Norms for Lunch"

I vividly remember the enforcement of norms at a beverage distribution company. I was conducting a group interview with some warehouse workers just before lunchtime. As the session wound down, the discussion turned to eating lunch. I asked if I could join the group for lunch. They readily agreed, and I was treated like one of the guys throughout the discussion of sports, automobiles, dating, ex-wives . . . and other guy stuff.

What was most interesting to me, as an OC consultant, was the end of lunch. About 55 minutes into lunch one of the younger guys said, "We had better get back to work — our hour is almost up." One of the unofficial leaders said, "Nonsense! Everybody knows we get an extra five minutes. Are you trying to make the rest of us look bad?" Nobody moved.

It was interesting for me to watch every guy in the group clock-in at one hour and five minutes. My subsequent timecard research proved interesting. Popular people took one hour and five minutes for lunch; unpopular people took one hour or less. Coincidence? Were norms driving behavior in this organization?

The next deeper level involves **values**. Values determine what is important (quality vs. quantity, individual vs. team success, or creativity vs. conformity). Careful analysis will reveal how the company's norms are driven by these values.

At the deepest level we find the taken-for-granted, **basic assumptions**. These basic assumptions become implicit and unquestioned. These are assumptions about "the way things are" (business, human nature, the meaning of success).

The reason changing organizational cultures is so difficult is the fact that they are rooted in this dark, unexamined level of basic assumptions. Questioning these basic assumptions ("the unquestionable") creates great anxiety for many organizational members. Frequently, the resulting frustration and anger are aimed at the OC consultant (the one doing the questioning).

Organizational Culture and Organizational Success

Numerous studies have revealed the relationship between organizational culture and organizational performance (Denison, 1989; Kotter & Heskett, 1992).

Some companies with extraordinary returns (including Southwest Airlines and Wal-Mart with returns of 20,000%) have outperformed their rivals without the traditional competitive advantages. "The major distinguishing feature in these companies, their most important competitive advantage, the most powerful factor they all highlight as a key ingredient in their success, is their organizational culture" (Cameron & Quinn, 1999).

Trice and Beyer (1993) believe a strong, unique organizational culture provides the following benefits:

1. reduces collective uncertainties

2. creates social order

3. creates community

4. creates a collective identity and commitment

5. establishes a vision for the future

Organizational Culture and Organizational Change

Organizational change efforts will fail if organizational culture remains fundamentally the same. The effectiveness of organizational change efforts requires embedding the improvement strategies in a cultural change (Cameron & Quinn, 1999; Cameron, Freeman, & Mishra, 1991).

Changes in procedures remain superficial and short-lived unless there are fundamental changes in values, ways of thinking, and approaches to problem solving. The resisting forces (discussed in Lewin's Forcefield Analysis) will renew their efforts to re-establish the old status quo. Cameron and Quinn (1999, p.10) found in these scenarios that "organizations may be worse off than had the change strategy not been attempted in the first place."

Cameron and Quinn (1999, p.13) conclude their discussion on the power of culture change by saying, "The status quo will prevail. We repeat! Without culture change, there is little hope of enduring improvement in organizational performance."

Cameron & Quinn's "Types"

Before discussing how to diagnose organizational culture, let's look at Cameron and Quinn's (1999) model of organizational culture. The four types of organizational culture in their model are:

1. the clan
2. the adhocracy
3. the market
4. the hierarchy

The clan culture is like an extended family. The leader is frequently a parental figure. The glue that holds the clan together is loyalty or tradition. Success is defined in terms of sensitivity to people (customers and employees). Many Japanese and Mexican firms have a clan culture.

The adhocracy features temporary team membership and constantly changing structure. Success is seen in terms of creativity and new ideas. Effective leadership is seen as visionary, innovative, and risk-oriented (Cameron & Quinn, 1999). Many high-tech firms have this type of culture.

The market culture is market-driven and highly competitive. Success is seen in terms of market share and market penetration. Effective leaders are seen as tough, demanding, and hard-driving. Insurance and other sales-oriented companies typically have a market culture.

The hierarchy is formal and highly structured. Success is defined in terms of efficiency. Effective leaders establish and monitor policies and procedures for lower costs and tighter scheduling. Large consumer-products manufacturers are typically examples of hierarchies.

The organization's life cycle can affect its culture. Some companies start as adhocracies, become a clan with the founder as the parent figure, grow into a hierarchy, and finally adopt a market culture to survive in competition with younger competitors.

Cameron and Quinn's OCAI Instrument

Cameron and Quinn (1999) have developed an organizational diagnostic tool called the Organizational Culture Assessment Instrument (OCAI). The OCAI has been used in more than a thousand organizations. The instrument, in the form of a questionnaire, gathers individual assessments of six key dimensions of organizational culture:

1. dominant characteristics
2. organizational leadership
3. management of employees
4. organizational glue
5. strategic emphases
6. criteria for success

Each participant assesses the organization on the six aspects twice: first, based on the current (now), and then based on a desired future (preferred). Each of the six questions allows for the allocation of 100 points over four alternatives. This ipsative rating scale permits the respondent to indicate the existence of more than one culture, in varying degrees. For example, all four cultures may exist in one organizational aspect in the following percentages: 60, 25, 10, and 5. Scoring is simple. Simply add all the A's, divide by six. Then the B's, and so forth. The results can then be plotted on a graph.

Cameron & Quinn's Organizational Profiles

By plotting the responses to Cameron and Quinn's OCAI questions on a four-quadrant graph (Cameron & Quinn, 1999, p.59) a visual (two kite-like shapes) of the current culture versus the preferred future culture is created. Many executives suddenly realize how much work will be needed when they see the visual presentation. Only after seeing this visual are some executives ready to talk about culture change taking years.

Of course, the participants will all have different assessments, so a group consensus must be arrived at before strategies for change can be considered. Coming to this consensus is typically a valuable exercise.

Very large differences between current and preferred cultures require more radical changes and longer periods of time. The radical changes include terminating employees who are deeply rooted in the old culture.

Schein's Approach

Schein's (1992) approach to diagnosing organizational culture differs in many ways from Cameron and Quinn's (1999), but both approaches share important similarities. Both assume leadership plays an important role in creating, diagnosing, and changing organizational culture. Both assume the OC consultant must facilitate the process of making implicit assumptions explicit.

Schein (1992) is critical of the overuse of cultural surveys/questionnaires. He believes culture surveys/questionnaires only create another artifact "subject to the same interpretation problems as other artifacts" (p.186).

Schein (1992, p.148) makes several insightful statements. Let's consider a few of them here:

1. "Culture is a set of shared assumptions; hence obtaining the initial data in a group setting is appropriate and valid."
2. Not all parts of the culture are relevant.
3. "Insiders are capable of understanding and making explicit the tacit assumptions . . . but they need outsider help in the process."
4. Group members must be able to categorize assumptions into "aids" and "hindrances."

Schein's (1992) approach follows these steps and substeps:

Step 1 — Obtaining Leadership Commitment

Step 2 — Conducting a Large Group Meeting

Substep 2a — Consultant gives a short lecture on what culture is, and how it is created.

Substep 2b — Eliciting descriptions about artifacts (dress codes, general and specific behaviors, physical layout, use of time and space, expressed/unexpressed emotions). Everything is written on flipchart paper and taped to the walls. The visuals help stimulate deeper thinking about the culture.

Substep 2c — Identifying espoused values, starting with the artifacts of most interest to the group. Consultant asks "the reasons why they do what they do" (p.152). Separate flipchart sheets should be used for values. Disagreements should be discussed.

Substep 2d — Making a "First Cut" at Shared Underlying Assumptions can be derived from the lists of artifacts and values on the walls. "Important and salient assumptions are ones that trigger a whole new set of insights and new data, that begin to make sense of a whole range of things that they do and espouse" (p.153).

Step 3 — Identifying Cultural Aids and Hindrances in Subgroups. Subgroups have two tasks: first, refine assumptions and identify other assumptions; second, categorize assumptions into "aid" or "hinder." The subgroup should prepare a report with two or three assumptions that aid and two or three assumptions that hinder.

Step 4 — Consensus and Joint Analysis. This step begins with the reports from the subgroups. The entire group should then work toward consensus on important shared assumptions, and then consensus on implications of those assumptions. A discussion should follow concerning the role of each assumption in aiding or hindering what the group wants to accomplish.

Step 5 — Develop the Change Strategy. This step may be done with the entire group or in subgroups.

Ethnographic vs. Clinical Approaches

Schein (1992) makes a clear distinction between the ethnographic approach and the clinical approach to studying organizational culture. These arguments (discussions) take place between university faculty members every day. Research professors claim to be more scientific because they study a phenomenon and leave it the way they found it. Frankly, as a practitioner (a clinician), I have little interest in conducting this kind of research. I see the value of "pure research," but I have a different motivation.

As an OC practitioner, I conduct "applied research" or action research. Kurt Lewin, the model of an applied social scientist, once said, "Action research should involve no research without action, and no action without research." This is profound advice for the OC consultant.

My colleagues who are research professors pride themselves on **not** taking any money from the subject organization. They believe that refusing money keeps them objective.

As a practitioner, I take money from my client organizations. I believe the money indicates their motivation to solve organizational problems. Simply being invited to take a look at the organization does not indicate a desire to change anything (it does not even recognize a problem). I want motivated clients who are willing to work hard with me in diagnosing problems and designing interventions. I believe the desire to solve existing problems is essential for organizational change.

I agree with Schein (1987, 1992) when he writes, "only a joint effort between an insider and an outsider can decipher the essential assumptions and their patterns of interrelationships" (1992, p.169). Even highly motivated clients will not be able to spontaneously discuss their organization's "basic assumptions and how they are patterned because they have dropped out of awareness and are taken for granted" (1992, p.170). A collaborative effort is needed to overcome the client's lack of awareness.

A Collaborative Approach

It is essential for the OC consultant to find motivated client members. They are a prerequisite for the successful analysis of what's going on in the organization. Motivated client members are ready to hear the consultant's theories and hunches without getting defensive.

The really important data is in the client's head, so the consultant must work hard to establish an open, trusting, helping relationship to get to that information. Once a hypothesis is developed, the consultant and client "must determine what additional data would constitute a valid test of whether such an assumption is operating" (Schein, 1992, p.174).

Schein (1992) believes the diagnosis should culminate in a written description of the assumptions and how they relate to each other in a meaningful pattern. The written description may be modified, but it is essential that consultant and client agree on the assumptions and how they are patterned.

What to Ask

Schein offers several questions to ask the client to stimulate cultural thinking. Here are a few of his questions:

1. What's the history of the organization?
2. What were the values and goals of the founder and early leaders of the organization?
3. What have been some of the critical problems (survival problems) faced by the organization? How were they solved? Who solved them?

The key, of course, is to look for patterns. "We cannot argue that we are dealing with a cultural element until we see some repetition of response; some behaviors, values, and assumptions that clearly are shared and continue to be used in new situations" (Schein, 1992, p.179).

Organizational Culture and Leadership

Cameron and Quinn (1999) and Schein (1992) agree that leadership plays a critical role in creating and maintaining organizational culture.

Cameron and Quinn (1999) have developed an instrument called the Management Skills Assessment Instrument (MSAI) that can be used in an organization along with their Organizational Cultural Assessment Instrument (the OCAI was discussed earlier). Cameron and Quinn's MSAI profile is "based on the same framework as the organization culture profile, and can be used to identify which skills and competencies managers must develop or improve in order to enhance the culture change effort" (p.106). The MSAI is used in the University of Michigan's Management of Managers' Program (rated one of the top five executive education programs in the U.S.).

The MSAI is a 360-degree instrument completed by the manager, supervisor, peers, and subordinates. Completed data sheets are faxed to Behavioral Data Services in Ann Arbor, Michigan and returned to the consultant.

The MSAI gives feedback on how successful a manager will be in the four types of organizational culture (clan, adhocracy, market, or hierarchy). Some managers may subsequently decide that the new organizational culture is not for them and leave the organization. This reaction could be a good result. Major changes in organizational culture will require major changes in member behavior.

Schein (1978, 1983, 1992) emphasizes the importance of the founder in culture formation. In addition to high levels of self-confidence and determination, he or she typically has strong assumptions about the nature of the world, the role of the organization, the nature of human beings and relationships, how truth is determined, and how to manage space and time (Schein, 1992, p.213).

The process of culture formation is linked to organizational formation. A founder with a vision is joined by one or more people who share the founder's vision and commitment. Large amounts of time, energy, and money are invested in the new venture. If success is obtained, the members assume their assumptions are right. The assumptions are taught to new members. The shared history of the members lead to shared assumptions about right and wrong, good and bad.

Transmitting Culture

Once the fledging organization becomes stable as a result of a series of successes, the dynamics change. New members are socialized into the "right" way of doing things.

Schein (1992) believes there are "six primary embedding mechanisms" and "six reinforcing mechanisms." The six **primary** embedding mechanisms (p.231) are:

1. What leaders pay attention to, measure, and control.
2. How leaders react to critical incidents and crises.
3. How scarce resources are allocated.
4. Deliberate role modeling and teaching.
5. Allocation of rewards and status.
6. Recruitment, selection, promotion, and excommunication.

Without going into detail here, it is plain to see how these mechanisms weave (whether consciously or unconsciously) the leaders' basic assumptions into the culture.

Schein (1992, p.231) also lists six **reinforcing** mechanisms. These reinforcing mechanisms only work "if they are consistent with the primary mechanisms" (discussed above).

1. organizational design and structure
2. organizational systems and procedures
3. organizational rites and rituals
4. design of physical environment
5. stories, legends, and myths
6. statements of philosophy, values, and creed

Schein (1992) believes managers can consciously use these mechanisms to build the desired culture. He states, "What the manager must recognize is that all of the primary mechanisms must be used, and all of them must be consistent with each other" (p.253).

Changing Organizational Culture

Despite its deeply ingrained nature, organizational culture will (and does) change. It is a slow process, but it happens spontaneously (or according to a plan) in all organizations. Spontaneous change is frequently less painful, if it is slow and non-threatening.

On the other hand, planned change is often seen as forced and threatening. The benefits of planned change must be sold to the troops. Then, senior management must be prepared for a frustratingly slow process as it implements all of the mechanisms suggested by Schein above.

Organizational culture change is usually in response to a crisis. "The traditional interpretation and behavior patterns are no longer successful" (Schreyoegg, Oechsler, & Waechter, 1995). New behaviors and thinking can then be introduced. Resistance to change breaks down as successes result from the new ways.

Cameron and Quinn (1999) offer a few helpful hints for change agents:

1. Find something easy to change first. Change it and celebrate.
2. Build coalitions of supporters (including opinion leaders).
3. Set targets for incremental completions.
4. Share information about the changes (reduce rumors, provide information).
5. Define how results will be assessed.
6. Make clear the advantages of change.
7. Reward the new desired behaviors.
8. Change reinforcing mechanisms (selection, appraisal systems, promotion criteria, and reward systems).

Summary

Organizational cultural change can be slow and frustrating, but the benefits can include dramatically improved organizational performance. The OC consultant should be prepared to facilitate this process.

REFERENCES

Cameron, K.S., Freeman, S.J., & Mishra, A.K. (1991). Best practices in white-collar downsizing: Managing contradictions. *Academy of Management Executive*, 5, 57-73.

Cameron, K.S. & Quinn, R.E. (1999). *Diagnosing and changing organizational culture.* Reading, MA: Addison-Wesley.

Denison, D. (1997). *Corporate culture and organizational effectiveness.* New York: John Wiley.

Kotter, J.P. & Heskett, J.L. (1992). *Corporate culture and performance.* New York: Free Press.

Schein, E.H. (1978). *Career dynamics: Matching individual and organizational needs.* Reading, MA: Addison-Wesley.

Schein, E.H. (1983). The role of the founder in creating organizational culture. *Organizational Dynamics*, Summer, pp.13-28.

Schein, E.H. (1987). *The clinical perspective in fieldwork.* Newbury Park, CA: Sage.

Schein, E.H. (1992). *Organizational cultural and leadership* (2nd ed.). San Francisco: Jossey-Bass.

Schreyoegg, G., Oechsler, W., & Waechter, H. (1995). *Managing in a European context.* Wiesbaden, Germany: Gabler.

Trice, H. & Beyer, J. (1993). *The cultures of work organizations.* Englewood Cliffs, NJ: Prentice-Hall.

CHAPTER 10

Human Process Interventions

The next three chapters will be devoted to process interventions. As stated in Chapter 1, there are human process interventions and technical process interventions. Since the work of OC consultants includes facilitating human process interventions, we will discuss several (but by no means all) of these interventions.

In this chapter we will discuss team-building and conflict-management interventions. In Chapter 11 we will cover management development interventions. In Chapter 12 we will review the most effective organizational learning interventions.

As emphasized throughout this book, the OC consultant's primary purpose is to facilitate the work of aligning the organization's structure, culture, and human processes with the organization's strategic plan. Human processes in an organization involve "how" things get done. Fortunately, one of the best developed areas of OC practice is in the area of human process interventions.

Let's look first at some team-building interventions, and then we'll examine some interventions specifically designed for conflict management.

Team-Building Interventions

Many organizations have switched to team-based work structures to implement their new market-driven strategic plans. The use of cross-functional teams has been highly effective in some situations, but disastrous in others.

Most individuals in Western societies, especially in the U.S., have received very little training in how to work effectively in teams. Thus, team building interventions have become a valuable professional service offered by OC consultants. Clients typically do not have to be convinced about the importance of enhancing team effectiveness.

Research tells us that effective teams have the following characteristics:

1. a clear mission and action plan
2. an informal, comfortable atmosphere
3. open communication
4. full participation
5. civil disagreement
6. clear role expectations
7. healthy external relationships, and
8. acceptance of style diversity.

The OC consultant should be concerned if these characteristics don't exist in his/her client's teams. This checklist can be shared with the team, since the implications are rather obvious.

Additional research on high-performance work teams (HPWTs) is also helpful. HPWTs are described as teams that have been recognized by others as being extraordinarily effective. What appears to separate the HPWTs from other effective teams is **personal commitment** among the members. HPWT members demonstrate a personal commitment to each other's growth and success.

Clearly, HPWTs are not created overnight.

PRACTICE LOG 10.1 An HPWT

For many years I have conducted workshops for groups of executives and professionals. Over the years, I have had several colleagues work with me in a tag-team type instructor format. Some of these teams have been very effective (some have been disappointing).

One colleague and I seemed to be especially effective together. Our workshop participants often commented on how well Susan (not her real name) and I worked together.

After one workshop, Susan made a surprisingly negative comment about my performance. I was so shocked I didn't know how to respond.

I simply said "OK," and walked off.

As I sat alone at dinner that evening, I was feeling hurt about the comment. *Why would Susan say something like that? I thought we were friends?* I pondered the possible motivations for her comment.

What does she gain by putting me down? *Nothing.* Hasn't she always been concerned about me in the past? *Yes.*

It suddenly hit me. Susan's comment was for my own good! If she didn't care, she would have said nothing at all. I spent the rest of my dinner time thinking about how to change my presentation.

The next day, the response by the executive team to our presentation was amazing. The executives actually gave us a spontaneous standing ovation! Thanks Susan for the input!

We were an HPWT!

There are basically three types of team-building interventions with three distinct foci: diagnostic, process, and relationship:

a. team diagnostic interventions — help to increase awareness of group problems and opportunities (e.g., the Group Diagnostic Meeting)

b. team process interventions — are designed to improve communication, role expectations, decision making, goal setting (e.g., the Role Analysis Exercise)

c. team relationship interventions — are designed to build or strengthen relationships between boss and subordinates, or peers, or groups (e.g., the Appreciations & Concerns Exercise)

Let's begin by examining a generic team-building exercise that can be used with almost any group. Then we will look at various team-building interventions that are currently being used by OC consultants.

A Generic Team-Building Intervention

1. consultant interviews group members and leader

2. consultant categorizes data into themes

3. consultant feeds back themes (findings)

4. group prioritizes the themes (into an agenda)
5. group examines underlying dynamics of problems
6. group brainstorms alternative solutions
7. group develops an action plan

Group Diagnostic Meetings

The Action Research Model suggests completing diagnosis by the end of step three. While most OC practitioners would agree, many consultants also recognize the powerful team-building effect of getting the group members to diagnose their own problems together.

The purpose of the Group Diagnostic Meeting Intervention is to conduct a general critique of group performance. The purpose is **not** to find solutions, but simply to uncover and identify problems.

Several critical questions should be discussed:

1. What's the mission/purpose of the group?
2. How are we doing? (tasks, relationships, processes)
3. What are our opportunities and threats?
4. What are our strengths and weaknesses?

There are various ways to organize these discussions. For small groups, it is possible to discuss the issues with the entire group. In a large group, it may be helpful to break up into several "buzz" groups (subgroups of four to six members), and then to reconvene to share findings.

I know one consultant who uses one-on-one interviews. He has members interview each other using an interview guide with the four questions listed above. Then the participants reconvene to share lessons learned.

There are several advantages to using the Group Diagnostic Meeting Intervention:

1. an obvious team-building, "energizing" effect,
2. additional insight to support the typical diagnostic process (Action Research steps 1 thru 3), and

3. enhanced member buy-in for the interventions chosen.

Some organizations now use periodic (semi-annual or annual) Group Diagnostic Meetings to serve as group performance evaluations, similar to periodic performance evaluations for individual employees.

The Role Analysis Exercise

Warning! This exercise should be used only after careful diagnosis. The Role Analysis Exercise is **not** appropriate when there is a high level of conflict. (The Role Negotiation Intervention, discussed in the Conflict Management section of this chapter, would be more appropriate for high levels of conflict.)

The Role Analysis Exercise is designed to clarify the role expectations for the job incumbent. It also helps clarify how other roles in the group or department relate to (and support) the target job. The goal of the exercise is to work through differences in expectations.

The Role Analysis Exercise is especially important for new teams because it results in consensual agreement on expectations for each job/role on the team. It can also be used with more established teams, if clarification of role expectations is necessary.

The steps in the Role Analysis Exercise are as follows:

1. incumbent lists expectations of **target role**
2. group members add and delete
3. group members and incumbent agree on expectations
4. incumbent lists expectations of **other roles**
5. group members add and delete
6. group members and incumbent agree on expectations
7. incumbent writes the role profile
8. group members approve

This exercise involves a discussion of all related roles, not just the target role.

Interdependency Exercise

The Interdependency Exercise is used for three primary purposes:

1. getting people acquainted
2. bringing problems to the surface
3. providing insight into the problems ("challenges") of others

Here is an example of how to use this exercise with a group of ten organizational members:

1. Seat five members on each side of the table.
2. Have side A (members 1, 2 ,3, 4, & 5) interview the side B member (members 6, 7, 8, 9, & 10) who is sitting directly across the table with an interview guide (interdependency questions based on earlier diagnosis).
3. After ten minutes, shift line A one seat to interview the next individual.
4. Complete five interviews; take a break.
5. Then interview in pairs on the same side of the table. (If there is an odd number — use a combination of interviewer, interviewee, and observer.)

As with the Role Analysis Exercise, your diagnosis should indicate low levels of conflict. High levels of conflict here are difficult for the OC consultant to manage because so many interviews are happening simultaneously.

The Interdependency Exercise creates large amounts of data for group discussion. It can be a very effective team builder.

The Interdependency Exercise can also be used with very large groups (50 or more) by dividing the group into clusters of ten. It is also possible to use "question experts" (individuals responsible for one particular question) to gather and report findings back to the entire group.

Responsibility Charting

Responsibility Charting is helpful in clarifying who is responsible for what. The process is quite simple and usually generates much discussion.

Begin by constructing a grid. Down the left-side of the grid, list the decisions or tasks that must be accomplished (e.g., Decision/Task # 1, Decision/Task # 2, etc.) Across the top, list the "actors." In each resulting box each participant can indicate the responsibility of each actor.

I prefer to use five classes of behavior:

R — responsible for initiating action and seeing that it gets carried out

A/V — must approve or veto

S — provides resources or support

I — must be informed

N — not involved

Invariably, differences come out about the responsibility of the different actors or players. This result leads to very helpful discussion about how things get done.

Let me make the following suggestions about using Responsibility Charting:

1. Assign an "R" (responsibility) to only one person. One individual should be ultimately responsible.

2. Avoid having too many people with approval/veto power. Most efficient operations require speed (of course, there are exceptions).

3. Any "S" (support role) should be explained. What type of support is involved (money, people, materials, information).

Appreciations & Concerns Exercise

The Appreciations and Concerns Exercise can be used when interview data reveals a lack of appreciation and an avoidance of confrontation. Like the Role Analysis Exercise, this should only be used for minor conflict. Again, proper diagnosis is necessary before choosing interventions.

The exercise follows these steps:

1. Each member jots down three appreciations of each member.

2. Each member jots down one or two minor (work-related) concerns.

3. One individual volunteers to listen to other members. Try to set a

good tone by getting the senior member of the group to volunteer.

4. Each member listens in turn. (I typically go around the table in a round-robin fashion, starting with the most senior member.)

Most group members are willing to listen to minor concerns after they have heard three positives. I am always amazed at how much "positives" mean to individuals. Perhaps we need to express them on a regular basis!

Forcefield Analysis

We discussed Kurt Lewin's Forcefield Analysis theory in Chapter 2. Here we want to talk about Forcefield Analysis as an intervention or "tool."

The participants should follow these steps:

1. Describe the current situation. (What is the status quo?)
2. Describe the desired situation. (What do we want the situation to be?)
3. Identify the driving forces. (What forces are driving toward the desired situation?)
4. Identify the resisting forces. (Who/what benefits from the current status quo?)
5. Examine the strengths of the forces. (Which ones are susceptible to change?)
6. Develop strategies to move the equilibrium/status quo. Add to the driving forces or reduce the resisting forces. (Remember, Lewin recommended the latter.)
7. Implement the action plan.
8. Institutionalize (refreeze) the new equilibrium.

In some situations the OC consultant may want to conduct this exercise anonymously. For example, if one of the resisting forces is one of the participants in the meeting, the discussion could get ugly. In this case, the OC consultant can gather the data, then report it back to the group.

"Visioning"

"Visioning," as it is typically called by OC consultants, is an activity that takes place at a strategic planning retreat, but it is also a very effective team building exercise. As group members share their visions, they begin to better understand their colleagues.

Visioning follows these steps:

1. Individuals write down characteristics of the future they want to see (e.g., products, services, HR practices, supplier relationships, leadership style, organizational structure).

2. Individual visions are written on flipchart paper, then posted on the walls.

3. Subgroups extract themes from the individual visions, then develop a subgroup vision.

4. Subgroup visions are shared with entire group.

5. Entire group agrees on a vision for the organization.

Organizational Mirror Intervention

The last team-building intervention I want to discuss is actually an inter-team intervention. Organizational Mirroring can be used for three or more teams/groups. This intervention includes a host group and representatives from other groups.

Here are the steps in Organizational Mirroring:

1. OC consultant interviews the group representatives (i.e., representatives from marketing, production, finance, and other departments).

2. OC consultant gathers (and organizes) the data received about the host group.

3. Leader of the host group (coached by the OC consultant) welcomes the representatives and invites open and frank comments.

4. The representatives are put in the "fishbowl." (The fishbowl is a small circle of chairs — for the representatives — in the middle of the room, which are surrounded by chairs for the host-group members.)

5. OC consultant feeds back perceptions of the host group, which were gathered in the interviews.

6. The representatives (while sitting in the fishbowl) discuss the comments about the host group. The OC consultant may ask questions to get the discussion started. The host-group members should only listen.

7. Then, the seating positions are switched. The host members sit in the fishbowl, while the representatives sit outside the fishbowl.

8. The host group members (while sitting in the fishbowl) discuss what they heard. They may ask questions only for clarification and/ or additional information.

9. Subgroups are formed, composed of host members and representatives, to identify the most important problems.

10. Groups reconvene to develop an action plan.

Conflict Management Interventions

Another important category of human process interventions is Conflict Management Interventions. Conflict is inevitable in organizations. A certain level of conflict (in the form of civil disagreement) actually enhances productivity. On the other hand, high levels of unresolved, unmanaged conflict can be enormously destructive.

Conflict management skills will become increasingly important in 21st century organizations for at least two reasons:

1. more diverse workforces (made up of workers from different cultures from throughout the world), and

2. the increasing use of cross-functional teams to work together on large projects and contracts.

As I stated earlier in this text, "the advantage of teams is diversity; the disadvantage of teams is diversity." The advantage and disadvantage are two sides of the same coin.

Cross-functional, diverse teams offer the important advantage of diverse viewpoints. While diverse viewpoints can lead to creative, innovative ideas, they almost invariably lead to conflict. However, conflict, like electricity, can improve our lives if it is managed in a responsible manner.

Since attempts to eliminate conflict lead to less creativity and productivity, let's think in terms of managing conflict. As with team-building interventions, many conflict management interventions are available to OC consultants.

Before jumping into the actual interventions for interpersonal and intergroup conflict, let's take a quick look at what we know about the characteristics of interpersonal and intergroup conflict.

First, we know that unresolved interpersonal or intergroup conflict gets worse if it is not dealt with. It is not likely to go away on its own.

Second, we also know that communication and interaction between the conflicting groups or parties tend to decline over time. This decline in interaction and communication leads to distorted beliefs about the other party or group. Each party or group begins to describe the other in negative stereotypic terms. Each party or group develops an us/them, good-guy/bad-guy viewpoint in which the other can do nothing right. Clearly, these scenarios deteriorate over time.

Researchers and practitioners tell us there are at least four basic strategies for dealing with interpersonal and intergroup conflict:

1. find a common enemy,
2. increase interaction/interdependency,
3. find a supraordinate goal (one that is too big for one party or group),
4. reduce competition.

Principled Negotiations

Principled Negotiations (Fisher, Ury, & Patton, 1991) is often touted as a conflict management method. Instead of thinking of it as a separate method, I prefer to think of it as "guidelines" for any conflict intervention.

Principled Negotiations emphasizes four items to focus on during any conflict intervention. It is important for the OC consultant to keep client members focused on:

1. the problem,
2. member interests (not positions),

3. multiple (not single) options,

4. objective criteria for agreement.

Let's look at each item, one at a time. First, it is important for the client members to separate the problem from the people. Members should clarify whether they are talking about perceptions, feelings, or hard data.

Second, the OC consultant should facilitate the disclosure of individual interests — what people actually want. This activity is more important than wasting time defending various conceptual positions.

Third, the OC consultant should insist on brainstorming that will provide multiple options to resolve the conflict. Multiple options allow the parties or groups to have free choice. Nobody wants to be forced into a corner.

Finally, specific objective criteria for an agreement should be determined. Important criteria may include cost, expediency, full participation, or other strategic priorities.

Let's look at a few popular conflict interventions. Remember, none of these interventions should be used until a proper diagnosis has been completed.

Blake, Shepard, and Mouton's Conflict Intervention

Blake, Shepard, and Mouton (1965) report success managing intergroup conflict with the following steps:

1. The consultant meets with the leaders of the two groups. The group leaders agree to work on a conflict intervention.

2. The consultant separates the two groups into two rooms, where the groups construct two lists:

   a. List One — "Don't Like List" — feelings and perceptions about the other group

   b. List Two — "What They Say About Us List" — predictions about what the other group is "saying about us"

3. Consultant reconvenes the group in one room and explains the "report with no discussion" rule. It is important for the client mem-

bers to simply **listen** to the other group.

4. Group A reads its "Don't Like List" out loud (these are the group's feelings and perceptions of the other group). Group B reads its "Don't Like List" out loud.

5. Group A reads its "What They Say About Us List" out loud. Group B reads its "What They Say About Us List" out loud.

6. Consultant sends the two groups to their separate rooms.

7. Groups discuss what they learned about themselves and the other group.

8. Groups construct a "Misperception/Miscommunication" list.

9. Groups construct an "Issues to be Resolved" list.

10. Groups reconvene and discuss "Misperception/Miscommunication" lists.

11. Groups discuss "Issues to be Resolved" lists.

12. Groups construct a Joint Action Plan.

TRW Conflict Intervention

The TRW Conflict Intervention (Fordyce & Weil, 1971) is similar to the Blake, Shepard, and Mouton Model. The TRW Model follows these steps:

1. The groups construct three lists.

    a. "Positive Feedback" — what one group likes about the other

    b. "Bug List" — what one group dislikes about the other

    c. "Empathy List" — predictions of what the other group "Says About Us"

2. Groups convene and read lists to each other.

3. Groups construct an agenda of "Prioritized Issues" together.

4. Temporary teams, containing members from each group, are formed to work on each item.

5. Temporary teams report back in a joint meeting.

6. Both groups develop an Action Plan together.

I have found both the Blake, Shepard, and Mouton (BS&M) Model and the TRW Model to be highly effective interventions for intergroup conflict. I tend to favor the BS&M Model for high levels of conflict, and the TRW Model when there is a relatively strong spirit of cooperation. I believe OC consultants should use steps from each model to design interventions that are appropriate for their client's situation.

Two-Person Contract Intervention

A very effective intervention for two-person conflict is the Two-Person Contract Intervention (French & Bell, 1999, p.185). This intervention involves three steps:

1. "Positives" List: Each party writes what he/she likes about the other. No negatives are allowed here. Consultant must emphasize understanding, not agreement.

2. "Pain/Resentment" List: Each party writes about **behaviors** causing hurt, anger, resentment, or embarrassment. Consultant must keep discussion focused on understanding, not debate or justification for behavior.

3. The Contract — an agreement involving the following statements:

   a. It would contribute to my effectiveness if you did more _____.

   b. It would contribute to my effectiveness if you did less _____.

   c. It would contribute to my effectiveness if you continued _____.

   d. I am willing to do _____ to contribute to your effectiveness.

This contracting step is similar to the "Role Negotiation" idea of each party's being willing to give up something. We will discuss the Role Negotiation intervention next.

Role Negotiation Technique

The Role Negotiation Technique is a controlled, highly structured negotiation used for individuals who are **unwilling** to work with the other party. This technique is appropriate when there are high levels of conflict.

The Role Negotiation Technique is based on the following assumptions:

1. People prefer a fairly negotiated settlement rather than unresolved conflict.

2. People will honor a contract in which they agree to change a behavior in exchange for a change by another person.

It is essential that the OC consultant maintain a controlled, highly structured atmosphere. A climate of anger or rage leads to defensiveness, not collaboration.

The consultant must establish the negotiating/contracting guidelines. This process includes setting the climate and clearly presenting the ground rules. The ground rules include the following:

1. Discussion must focus on work behaviors, not feelings about others.

2. Individuals must be specific about what they want. Universal concepts and theories must be replaced by specific requests.

3. All expectations must be in writing.

4. Any agreed-to change must be reciprocated.

Similar to the Two-Person Contract Intervention, the parties should write out what they want the others to do: more of, less of, or maintain. Each participant should write statements such as:

1. I want more of _____ from _____.

2. I want less of _____ from _____.

3. I want _____ to continue _____.

The negotiation phase requires strict supervision from the OC consultant. Each person **must** give something to get something. Reciprocity is essential in this technique.

Essentials of Conflict Management

There are many other conflict management interventions in use today, of course. But there are some essential processes used in all conflict management interventions. The first three on my list are essentials for the consultant:

1. Consultant optimizes the tension (a moderate level of tension should be maintained).

2. Consultant must focus discussion on specifics and clarity.

3. Consultant allows for differentiation before integration (negative feelings are aired before solutions are sought).

4. Both parties are motivated to resolve the conflict. Each party sees a benefit in resolving the conflict.

5. There must be a balance in situational power. One party must not be able to force compliance with his or her will.

6. A collaboratively developed action plan must be created by the parties. There must be buy-in on both sides.

Two Types of Conflict

Finally, it is important to keep in mind that there are two types of conflict: one based on communication and one based on substantive issues. I once heard a counselor say all marriage problems are communication problems. I disagree.

Many marriage problems, or any other relational problems, are communication problems. There are numerous techniques available for OC consultants to facilitate the resolution for communication problems. These techniques usually involve restructuring perceptions and/or empathetic listening.

Conflict based on substantive issues is quite different. Differences on substantive issues (beyond basic understanding of the other party's viewpoint) may require a negotiated settlement under which each party must give up something. In some situations, a negotiated settlement may not be acceptable to either party. Using marriage as an example, if the husband wants to live in New York and the wife wants to live in San Francisco, a compromise to live in Kansas City may not satisfy either party.

The OC consultant should be aware of the difference between the two types of conflict when diagnosing the data he or she has gathered from the client.

REFERENCES

Blake, R., Shepard, H., & Mouton, J. (1965). *Managing intergroup conflict in industry.* Houston, TX: Gulf Publishing.

Fisher, R., Ury, W., & Patton, B. (1991). *Getting to yes,* 2nd ed. New York: Penguin Books.

Fordyce, J.K. & Weil, R. (1971). *Managing with people.* Reading, MA: Addison-Wesley.

French, W.L. & Bell, C.H. (1999). *Organization development,* 6th ed. Upper Saddle River, NJ: Prentice-Hall.

CHAPTER 11

Management Development Interventions

Organizational change must be led by somebody. OC consultants are facilitators, not the leaders, of organizational change. Successful organizational change implementation requires effective leadership by managers.

The management development process of the organization warrants the careful attention of OC consultants. Managers become the leaders of the organization. Managers are responsible for implementing the company's strategy and for leading change initiatives.

In the model I share throughout this book, I emphasize the importance of the organization's structure, culture, and human processes supporting the organization's strategic plan.

Strategy	
Structure	Human Processes
Culture	

FIGURE 11.1

One critical human process in any organization is the management development process. Without a doubt, managers play a very important role in the organization. They are the role models and guides for other organizational members. Management development should be a high priority for the organization.

Countless books and articles have been written about training and development. Literally billions of dollars are spent annually on training and development.

It is important, for our purposes, to make a clear distinction between "training" and "development." Training involves the facilitation of

skills acquisition by organizational members. Skills, including how to run the widget-making machine, how to prepare financial reports, or how to calculate the costs involved in a specific manufacturing process, require training.

"Development" is aimed at the managers of the organization. Managers must possess the knowledge and attitudes to work with complex people and conceptual problems — under considerable pressure. The necessary managerial knowledge and attitudes can be acquired in a variety of ways.

It is important for organizations to think of management development systematically. Management development should not be simply hit-or-miss training sessions offered by outside vendors, or a bookshelf full of canned courses.

An effective management development system contains the following three elements:

1. assessment
2. development
3. performance management

Let's look at each element in detail.

Assessment

Management assessment, like other interventions, is concerned with "fit." To maximize organizational effectiveness and the individual manager's satisfaction, there must be a fit between the organization and the manager.

First and foremost, the manager must understand the organization in which he or she works. Managers must have a clear understanding of the organization's vision and strategy, its structure, its culture, and its processes. This allows the manager to focus his or her efforts on strategically important tasks.

The management assessment process should be designed to help the manager develop an awareness of his or her personal preferences, and an awareness of how he or she interacts with others. This awareness is critical for developing the manager's strengths and ameliorating his or her weaknesses.

In-House vs. External Assessment

Management assessment can be done in-house or by independent assessment firms. Typically, only large organizations have the budget and expertise to perform this function in-house. Many companies prefer to outsource this function to professional consultants or firms that conduct management assessments for a living.

Assessment Instruments

Management assessment involves the use of multiple assessment instruments that provide feedback for the purpose of increasing a manager's self-awareness.

Most of these instruments require consultant training and certification before purchasing and using. Certification of the consultant helps to assure both the organization and the manager of appropriate instrument use and interpretation.

I recommend not using free internet instruments that require the manager to interpret his or her data without guidance. Paying consultants who are certified to use and interpret instruments (instruments that have been subjected to rigorous validity studies) is a wise investment of the organization's money. Misinterpretation or invalid instruments do more harm than good.

Let me introduce you to a half-dozen of the instruments I currently use in practice. Please note that there are many more available to practitioners, but these six will be valuable tools in your consulting toolbox:

1. MBTI
2. FIRO Elements B
3. KAI
4. ABLE
5. SDLRS
6. CCAI

One of the best known of the assessment (or preference) instruments is the Myers-Briggs Type Indicator (MBTI). The MBTI provides the manager with awareness about his or her preferences in four areas:

1. external vs. internal world (extraversion/introversion)
2. how data is taken in (sensing/intuiting)
3. how decisions are made (thinking/feeling)
4. scheduling vs. spontaneity (judging/perceiving)

According to the original theory, developed by German-Swiss psychologist Carl Jung, extraverts (E) prefer the external world. Extraverts process information by talking about it. They are energized by people. Introverts (I) process information internally, by quietly thinking about it. Introverts have to get away from people to "recharge their batteries" (don't take it personally if you are an extravert).

Sensors (S) depend on their five senses. What they can see, hear, smell, touch, or taste is "real." They are focused on the here-and-now. Intuitors (N) are more concerned with ideas, concepts, and possibilities. They tend to focus on the future.

Thinkers (T) and feelers (F) make decisions differently. Thinkers work hard to develop logical, linear, rational arguments to support universal principles that should apply to everyone. Feelers believe that process is too cold. They want to talk about how individuals will be affected by the decisions. Thinkers don't like exceptions to the rules; feelers don't mind exceptions. Feelers believe decisions should be made on a case-by-case basis.

The judging (J) and perceiving (P) dichotomy is concerned with the use of time. Js want things to be highly structured; an agenda or to-do list is important to them. Ps believe the spontaneous use of time is best; agendas and to-do lists are restricting to them.

I usually use the MBTI first with clients, before moving on to other instruments. Most client members I've worked with find the MBTI interesting and fun. And because the MBTI has been subjected to rigorous reliability and validity testing, most managers don't argue with the feedback. The latest version, MBTI Form M, is especially well received by clients.

The FIRO Elements B is part of a series of instruments developed by Will Schutz. The Elements B is especially appropriate in management assessment. The Elements B offers feedback concerning how the manager prefers to interact with others. Like other preference instruments, this instrument does not measure skills; it simply reveals preferences.

The FIRO Elements B focuses on a manager's preferences for inclusion, control, and openness in human interactions. The instrument provides feedback on four aspects of each of these three preferences: two concerning "give" (now vs. wanted) and two concerning "receive" (now vs. wanted). Large differences between giving/receiving-now and giving/receiving-wanted indicate that the manager is experiencing stress concerning that particular aspect of human interaction.

The FIRO Elements B is also a great team-building tool. Since everybody has different needs/wants for inclusion, control, and openness, it is helpful to understand the needs/wants of other team members. I have used this instrument in practice with intact teams and new teams. With dysfunctional teams this instrument usually reveals large difference in either inclusion, control, or openness.

Another valuable tool in management assessment is the Kirton Adaptor/Innovator Instrument (KAI). Unfortunately, the KAI is still not widely used in the U.S. The KAI is the brainchild of Michael Kirton, a British researcher and practitioner.

Kirton believes all human beings are creative, but he believes they express their creativity differently based on how they prefer to change (improve) things. Adaptors (A) want to change things slowly, incrementally, one-step at a time. Adaptors like the tweaking involved in a continuous improvement (TQM) process. Innovators (I) like quick, quantum, dramatic change. Innovators like the idea of re-engineering or changing the whole system.

There are also "bridges," like me. Bridges score in the middle of Kirton's scale; they can appreciate both approaches. I have two close friends; they are both very intelligent. She is an adaptor; she wants slow, incremental, cautious change. He speaks in terms of "blowing up the system" and starting from scratch. I enjoy both of them, but they can't stand to be around each other.

The KAI is very helpful because it reveals potential problems between extreme adaptors and extreme innovators. Awareness of these differences allows for alternative responses.

There are several 360-degree management assessment instruments available. One inexpensive example is the Assessment of Basic Leader Effectiveness (ABLE), but in certain situations (particularly in senior management assessments) where more detail is needed, other instruments may be more appropriate. Most of these 360-degree instruments tend to be quite expensive because of the enormous amount of comparative reports that can be generated by the software.

A 360-degree assessment provides feedback from the manager's supervisor, subordinate, and peers. The feedback includes perceptions of the target manager's managerial skills. This is valuable input. Managers are often oblivious to their own counterproductive behaviors. Mangers need to be aware of any career-derailing behaviors.

The Self-Directed Learning Readiness Scale (SDLRS) is a valuable instrument in both management development and organizational learning (Beitler, 2000). I will discuss the SDLRS at length in the next chapter. For management development purposes, the SDLRS helps in designing a customized learning and development plan for the individual manager.

The Cross-Cultural Adaptability Index (CCAI) is becoming increasingly important in management development as companies become global organizations. I have done much work with my colleagues in preparing and supporting expatriate managers. Managers with low adaptability scores do poorly on foreign assignments, regardless of how talented or well-trained they are (Chuprina & Durr, 2001). I will discuss this issue further in the chapter on the globalization of organizations, management, and OC.

The last instrument I will mention here is Cameron and Quinn's

(1999) Management Skills Assessment Instrument (MSAI). Kim Cameron designed this instrument to provide the manager with a profile of his or her managerial competencies.

Cameron and Quinn (1999) are best known for their Organizational Culture Assessment Instrument (the OCAI was discussed in Chapter 8). The MSAI has the benefit of indicating the organizational culture that is the best fit for the manager.

The MSAI takes approximately 30 minutes to complete. The answer sheet is then faxed to Behavioral Data Services (BDS). BDS compiles the data into a customized report for the individual manager.

Development

Developmental activities for managers fall into several categories:

Coaching/Mentoring

Behavior Modeling

Experiential/Sensitivity Training

Job Rotation

Cross-Cultural Training

Career Planning

Coaching/Mentoring

Coaching provides guidance for specific skill development. The role of coach can be performed by a supervisor, peer, or consultant. OC consultants frequently serve as coaches for managers.

Mentoring is broader in focus than coaching. Mentoring usually involves an older (more experienced) manager taking a younger manager under his or her wing. Mentoring goes beyond specific skill development; it includes guidance for career and personal development. Successful mentoring involves a mentor who is personally committed to the success of a protégé. Effective mentoring relationships can be encouraged or supported by the company but not forced.

Behavior Modeling

Behavior modeling can be done with individual managers or with groups of managers. It is based on Bandura's (1977) Social Learning Theory. Social Learning Theory assumes the following about individuals:

1. they must perceive the connection between their behavior and certain outcomes,

2. they must desire the outcomes, and

3. they must believe they can accomplish them.

Behavior modeling involves:

1. discovering specific behaviors that lead to success,

2. watching a model demonstrate the behavior (the model must be somebody the manager can relate to), and

3. practicing the behavior under the guidance of the expert.

In behavior modeling sessions, videotaping can be used to capture role-playing exercises. The videotapes can then be reviewed and critiqued.

Experiential/Sensitivity Training

While the use of experiential and sensitivity training has declined in recent years, it may still have a place in some organizations. Since experiential or sensitivity exercises focus on non-work-related issues, proving transferability back to the job is difficult.

A popular form of sensitivity training during the 1970s was the T-group. T-groups were unstructured, agendaless group sessions where feelings and reactions of group members were openly discussed. The goals of the sessions included increased self-awareness, sensitivity to others, and improved communication.

Since T-groups frequently involve intense emotional reactions, I recommend against their use unless a trained psychologist facilitates the session. Generally speaking, T-groups are inappropriate for business or professional groups. Management development should not be confused with psychotherapy.

Other experiential exercises (such as wilderness journeys and white-water rafting) should be seen as fun, not necessarily developmental.

Job Rotation

One highly effective management development activity is job rotation. In job rotation (unlike T-groups) it is easy to see the transferability of the experience or new learning to actual job performance improvements. Job rotation provides the manager with not only new skills (running the widget-making machine), but new insights into the world of others (understanding the viewpoint of the widget-machine operator).

Cross-Cultural Training

Effective cross-cultural training is still lacking in American companies. Americans, true to their culturally insensitive stereotype, conduct cross-cultural training in an ethnocentric manner. Many of these American programs focus only on American issues (black/white, male/female). This narrow approach excludes much of the rest of the world.

I will have more to say about training managers for foreign (truly cross-cultural) assignments in the chapter on globalization. The failure rate of American expatriate managers is extremely high, and unacceptable. An effective program for expatriate manager preparation and support is critical to the global organization's success.

Career Planning

Career planning activities should be supported (financially and otherwise) by organizations because both the individual manager and the organization itself benefit. Managers who don't fit the organization or their jobs become increasingly dissatisfied and unproductive.

There are numerous career planning activities (Schein, 1987; Lippitt, 1970; Fordyce & Weil, 1971) available for managers. The purpose of these activities is to help the manager understand his or her core values. Core values are what are really important to the manager. Core values are powerful motivators.

Performance Management

Effective performance management systems for managers should include two related, well-planned subsystems:

1. goal setting and performance appraisal
2. rewards and guidance counseling

We will look first at goal setting and performance appraisals. Then, we will look at rewards to reinforce positive behavior and goal accomplishment. Finally, we will discuss the importance of providing guidance counseling for negative behavior and for failure to accomplish goals.

Goal Setting and Performance Appraisal

Performance appraisals should be based on collaboratively determined goals. Agreement on expectations must be reached during the goal setting phase. This collaborative process ensures the individual's buy-in. Actual performance should then be measured against these agreed-upon goals and expectations.

Performance appraisal should include both periodic (formal) and on-going (informal) feedback. Work-related successes, failures, strengths, and weaknesses should be discussed openly and frankly between the manager and his/her supervisor.

The use of performance appraisals is frequently driven by legal concerns but should be considered a developmental tool. Some experts (including Muchinsky, 2000) believe the traditional performance appraisal should involve two separate meetings: one for developmental purposes and one for administrative purposes (pay raises and related issues). I agree with Muchinsky's argument for two separate meetings. The developmental benefits of performance appraisals should not be overshadowed by administrative matters.

Performance evaluation provides two types of feedback: negative and positive. Negative feedback occurs when performance does not meet expectations and goals. Negative feedback should lead to discussion about future development. Positive feedback occurs when performance meets or exceeds expectations and goals. Performance at these levels should be reinforced by rewards.

Rewards and Guidance Counseling

"Reward systems are concerned with eliciting and reinforcing desired behaviors and work outcomes" (Cummings & Worley, 2001). "Desired" behaviors should be rewarded; undesired behaviors require guidance counseling. Let's discuss rewards for desired behaviors first.

The subject of rewarding and reinforcing behavior is closely related to the popular subject of motivation. Managers need more than managerial KSAs. Highly trained managers may still fail to meet their potential if they are not motivated.

Two types of rewards should be considered to enhance management performance: intrinsic rewards and extrinsic rewards. A combination of both can be found in effective reward systems.

The following examples of intrinsic rewards can be made available to most managers:

1. more decision-making authority
2. interesting assignments
3. enriched jobs

Managers are also motivated by the following extrinsic rewards:

1. pay increases and/or bonuses
2. stock options
3. gain sharing
4. promotions

Obviously, relying solely on extrinsic rewards is too expensive for companies in competitive industries. Intrinsic rewards preserve cash, plus they lead to long-term improvements in manager performance. Extrinsic rewards tend to produce only short-term performance improvements.

The key to finding motivating rewards is to identify the rewards that are most highly valued by the individual manager. For example, a flexible work schedule may be more motivating than a pay raise. Or an interesting job assignment (a lateral move) may be more motivating than a promotion. Identifying highly motivating rewards involves on-going communication with the individual manager. Each manager is motivated by different values.

Most companies still have reward systems designed by compensation experts or senior management. But "there is growing evidence that employee participation in the design and administration of a reward system can increase employee understanding and can contribute to feelings of control over and commitment to the plan" (Cummings & Worley, 2001).

While it is beyond the scope of this book, OC consultants should familiarize themselves with the wide variety of compensation options that are available, including:

1. skill-based pay
2. performance-based pay
3. gain sharing
4. "cafeteria-style" pay packages

Finally, senior managers must be willing and able to give constructive negative feedback to managers for whom they are responsible. All of us fail at times; all of us make mistakes. We can grow and learn from these failures and mistakes if we receive proper guidance. Serving subordinates in the role of a guidance counselor is an important managerial role. The organization should be confident that managers are prepared to perform in that role.

Summary

The organization's management development system should help align individual manager efforts with the organization's goals and strategic plan. It is critical that managers understand and support the organization's strategy, structure, culture, and processes.

REFERENCES

Bandura, A. (1977). *Social learning theory.* Englewood Cliffs, NJ: Prentice-Hall.

Beitler, M.A. (2000). Contract learning in organizational learning and management development. In H.B. Long & Associates (Eds.), *Practice and theory in self-directed learning.* Schaumburg, IL: Motorola University Press.

Cameron, K.S. & Quinn, R.E. (1999). *Diagnosing and changing organizational culture.* Reading, MA: Addison-Wesley.

Chuprina, L. & Durr, R. (2001). Implications of foreign culture and SDL on expatriate managers at Motorola, Inc. In H.B. Long & Associates (Eds.), *Self-directed learning in the new millennium.* Schaumberg, IL: Motorola University Press.

Cummings T.G. & Worley, C.G. (2001). *Organization development and change* (7th ed.). Cincinnati, OH: South-Western.

Fordyce, J.K. & Weil, R. (1971). *Managing with people.* Reading, MA: Addison-Wesley. (pp.109-113)

Lippitt, G. (1970). Developing life plans. *Training and Development Journal,* May, pp.2-7.

Muchinsky, P.M. (2000). *Psychology applied to work* (6th ed.). Belmont, CA: Wadsworth/ Thomson Learning.

Schein, E.H. (1987). Individuals and careers. In J.W. Lorsch (Ed.), *Handbook of organizational behavior.* Englewood Cliffs, NJ: Prentice-Hall.

CHAPTER 12

Organizational Learning Interventions

In the 21st century, leading companies in every industry will be knowledge-driven. To maintain a leadership position (or to merely survive in some industries) an organization must continually create or acquire knowledge, store knowledge, and transfer knowledge throughout the organization.

Unfortunately, an in-depth discussion of organizational learning (OL) and knowledge management (KM) interventions is beyond the scope of this book. For our purposes here, we will briefly discuss the OL and KM interventions that are currently available. All managers and organizational change consultants should be aware of these important human process interventions. For a detailed discussion of OL and KM interventions see my book entitled *Strategic Organizational Learning* (Beitler, 2005).

What is Organizational Learning?

Everybody agrees that organizational learning (OL) is important; many authors have said it is critical for organizational **survival**. While there are real threats in this area, there are also exciting opportunities. A well-crafted and implemented organizational learning plan can dramatically improve productivity.

Suppose we could create a workforce that was 10 to 20 percent more productive than the competitors' workforces. It's possible. That would give us a *sustainable competitive advantage*, an advantage that competitors could not quickly duplicate. It's possible, but not easy.

Creating a "learning organization" takes planned interventions that change the structure, culture, and processes of the organization. It may even require changing the strategic plan or changing the organization's mission itself.

The term "organizational learning" is not new. Argyris and Schön (1976) popularized it a quarter-century ago, but the term is used differently by different people. Some see it as the aggregate of individual learning that takes place in an organizational setting. Some see OL as learning that is embedded in the organization's policies, operations, and culture. Still others see OL as a mystical combination of the aggregate learning of individuals embedded in some Jungian-type of organizational collective unconscious. These three conceptualizations leave most senior managers cold.

We need practical working definitions to be able to communicate with our clients. In my earlier works I offered the following definition:

"Organizational learning is the organization's capacity to create or acquire new knowledge, and then develop that knowledge for the benefit of the organization."

Organizational learning, with its social science approach, is typically viewed by organizations as a human resource (HR) function. The OL efforts in the organization are usually the responsibility of the Chief Learning Officer (CLO).

What is Knowledge Management?

Knowledge management (KM) in American companies typically takes an IT approach. (In European companies KM includes organizational learning, and takes a social science approach.)

KM interventions focus on changing the technical processes the organization uses to collect, organize, and disseminate knowledge. KM utilizes electronic forms of information storage and transmission, such as intranets and data warehousing. KM, with its IT approach, is typically viewed by organizations as an IT function, thus KM is usually the responsibility of the Chief Technology Officer (CTO) or Chief Information Officer (CIO).

What is a Learning Organization?

The concept of a learning organization was popularized by Peter Senge (1990) in the early 1990s, but to date, no widely accepted definition has emerged. So, let me offer the following composite definition:

> "A learning organization is an organization that promotes, rewards, and captures individual learning for the benefit of the organization."

A learning organization in the twenty-first century will not only utilize traditional training and development, but a host of other OL and KM interventions.

With the above definition in mind, let's look at a variety of ways (interventions) that an organization can use to promote, reward, and capture individual learning for the benefit of the organization.

Traditional Training

Authorities agree that traditional, trainer-directed, classroom training will continue to diminish in importance as a delivery method for organizational learning in the 21st century. While that is true, OC consultants still must understand when to recommend traditional training to drive organizational change and to improve organizational effectiveness.

Even though traditional training is decreasing in importance, traditional training practice and theory continue to shape how organizations think about learning. Billions of dollars are still budgeted for traditional training.

To be effective traditional training must go through four critical phases: assessing, designing, conducting, and evaluating. OC consultants will immediately see the similarities between the Four-Phase Training Model and the Action Research Model that is used in OC practice.

Assessing

Designing and conducting training without first assessing the needs of the organization, the job, and the individual trainees is a waste of organizational and individual resources (time, energy, and money).

The assessing phase should determine whether or not there is a training need at all. Keep in mind that training is not the answer for all performance problems. Performance problems may be rooted in KSA (knowledge, skills, attitudes) problems. But, performance problems may also be rooted in motivational problems or a host of other "environmental" problems.

The performance problems with non-training roots (motivational and environmental problems) can't be resolved with training. Thus, the first goal of the assessing phase is to distinguish between training and non-training needs.

Assuming we find training needs, the goal of the assessing phase becomes determining training *objectives*. These objectives will become the criteria for designing, conducting, and evaluating the training. The ultimate purpose of the assessment phase is to clearly define the **required** KSAs (knowledge, skills, and attitudes) of the job versus the **current** KSAs of the trainees.

During the assessing phase it is important to do an organizational analysis. The organizational analysis provides a context for understanding the required KSAs of the job. Context is crucial. For example, the position of Vice President of Customer Relations for 3M Corporation has dramatically different expectations than the same job title at Wal-Mart Corporation.

Before we can properly design training, all three parts of the assessing phase (organizational, job, and individual) must be completed. The assessing phase does not end until written objectives have been agreed upon.

I would like to share one more OC-related thought about the assessment phase. During the assessment phase, you may discover that the problem is the design of the job itself. Obviously, a problem with job design cannot be corrected with training. If job design is your assessment of the problem, return to Chapter 8 and review our discussion about job structuring (or job design).

Designing

The success of the designing phase depends upon the written objectives determined during the assessing phase.

A major consideration during the design phase is organizational constraints. No organization has unlimited resources. Time, energy, and money must be efficiently and effectively allocated.

The design of training must facilitate learning and encourage the transfer of knowledge throughout the organization. Other design issues include attention, retention, and learning styles. No learning occurs until attention has been established. No learning will improve performance if it can't be retained. And training design should accommodate various learning styles.

The training design phase includes the process of choosing the most appropriate training method. Training methods can be categorized into three broad types: lecture w/discussion, games and simulations, and on-the-job training (OJT).

Lecture w/discussion is important to training design because virtually all training involves some lecture and some discussion. The appropriate use of all lecture or all discussion is rare. We need to use varying amounts of each depending on the training situation.

Games and simulations are designed to demonstrate various processes, and a large number of them are available: equipment simulators, business games, the in-basket technique, case studies, role playing, and behavior modeling. A detailed discussion of these is available in *Strategic Organizational Learning* (Beitler, 2005).

On-the-job training (OJT) is the most frequently used type of training. OJT is generally seen as cheap and informal. However, OJT is typically not cheap because there is a large opportunity cost involved in taking experienced workers away from their positions to conduct the training. Also, the informal nature of most OJT often leads to training that does not cover all of the critical aspects of the job.

The major advantage of OJT, of course, is "transfer" of the learning. Unlike some classroom training, OJT skills are highly relevant to the job.

Conducting

The conducting phase of training is the easiest, if you have properly completed the assessing and designing phases. Effectively conducting training only requires learning a few simple platform skills.

During the conducting phase of training, the most important trainer skill is that of questioning. Questioning has been used by great teachers throughout the ages. Socrates, the great ancient philosopher, led others to the truth by systematically asking one question after another. The Socratic method of questioning is still used in training today.

Trainers must know how to use both open-ended and closed-ended questions. Open-ended questions open up a discussion. They engage the trainees and allow for a re-direction of the training session toward topics of interest to the trainees. This can be very beneficial for learning. But, open-ended questions can lead to unpredictable responses. They often lead into a discussion of a topic that is not on the agenda. The trainer may have to use closed-ended questions to regain control of the session.

Closed-ended questions lead to specific answers. Asking "what are the five steps in a particular quality control procedure?" will result in a listing of the five steps...period. Closed-ended questions, in effect, close the discussion. The trainer must then be prepared to move on to another point.

Trainers must also be familiar with the use of a host of other types of questions: direct, overhead, reverse, and relay. Additionally, there are other platform skills available for dealing with introverted groups, know-it-alls, hostile trainees, and trainees who lack confidence. See Chapter 3 of *Strategic Organizational Learning* (Beitler, 2005) for a detailed discussion of platform skills.

Evaluating

Many trainers avoid the evaluating phase. Perhaps they don't want to see their mistakes receiving attention. But, good organizational management requires ongoing evaluation of all organizational activities.

When organizational resources are allocated to any activity, somebody must be responsible for those resources.

There are two types of training evaluation: outcome evaluation and process evaluation.

Outcome evaluation typically receives more attention from senior management. They want to compare planned outcomes with actual outcomes (results).

Process evaluation is critical for trainers and consultants. Process evaluation looks at data from before and during training. During process evaluation, the assessing, designing, and conducting phases are revisited to look for places to improve the process of the training.

Role of Traditional Training

While the percentage of overall corporate budgets for traditional training will continue to decline, it is essential that we understand traditional training theory and practice. Understanding traditional training theory and practice will help us to understand how organizational members view the "new" OL and KM interventions.

Self-Directed Learning

To remain competitive in the twenty-first century, self-directed learning must permeate the knowledge-driven organization. The culture of the 21st century learning organization must be one where every individual at every level is engaged in on-going, job-related learning. The traditional monthly or quarterly workshop will not suffice.

Unfortunately, the traditional syllabus-driven, teacher-directed school systems (particularly in the U.S.) encourage teacher-dependent, spoon-fed learning. Self-directed, self-initiated learning is a prerequisite for a learning organization to exist.

The environment for successful SDL and the environment for a flourishing learning organization share the same characteristics. Confessore and Kops (1998) found five characteristics reflected in both bodies of literature:

1. tolerance for errors, support for experimentation and risk taking, and an emphasis on creativity and innovation;

2. the use of a participative leadership style and delegation of responsibility to organizational members;

3. support for learning initiatives that are linked to the organization's goals and values;

4. encouragement of open communication and of information systems that provide for collaboration and teamwork, and the use of both internal and external learning resources; and,

5. provision of opportunities and situations for individual learning.

Over the past twenty-five years, an impressive body of literature has developed concerning the potential and practice of SDL. Tough (1979) speaks of *independent learning*—learning, for the most part, independent of teachers and institutions. Tough's approach to learning, with little or no institutional support, is also shared by the advocates of *distance learning* (e.g., Garrison, 1987). Knowles (1975) speaks of self-directed learning in institutional settings.

Long & The Guglielminos

While I found the work of Tough and Knowles to be inspiring, I had two reservations concerning the use of self-directed learning. Based on my own teaching, training, and consulting experience, I realized:

1) some intelligent adults are not psychologically equipped (or "ready") to succeed at self-directed learning, and

2) some subject matters (e.g., accounting) are not appropriate for self-directed learning.

My first concern was addressed in the works of Huey B. Long, and in the extensive research of Lucy and Paul Guglielmino with the self-directed learning readiness scale.

Long (1989, 1990, 1991) addresses the psychological aspects of SDL. Long (1989) depicts the successful self-directed learner as having the following characteristics: 1) self-confidence, 2) self-awareness, 3) self-reflectiveness, 4) a strong goal orientation, and 5) an aptitude for systematic procedures. Obviously, all organizational members do not exhibit these characteristics.

In his 1991 book chapter, entitled *Challenges in the Study and Practice of Self-Directed Learning*, Long presents his model in an illustration (p.22), divided into four quadrants that identify situations in which SDL is (and is not) appropriate based on the psychological make-up of the individual. It is important to note that Long (1991) prefers to speak in terms of degrees of individual self-direction, rather than in terms of "all-or-nothing" (p.15).

Measuring "readiness" for self-directed learning is the focus of the work of Lucy and Paul Guglielmino. As part of her dissertation work in 1977 at the University of Georgia, Lucy Guglielmino developed and field tested the Self-Directed Learning Readiness Scale, a Likert-type questionnaire with five response options per question (Guglielmino, 1978). The Self-Directed Learning Readiness Scale (SDLRS) was later expanded to its current 58 items. The SDLRS has become the most widely used instrument for assessment of self-directed learning readiness (Long & Ageykum, 1988; McCune, 1989; Merriam & Brockett, 1997). The self-scorable form for the SDLRS is called the Learning Preference Assessment (Guglielmino & Guglielmino, 1991a, 1991b).

Based on a compilation of more than 3000 respondents to the instrument, the Pearson split-half reliability of the English version is .94 (McCune, Guglielmino, Garcia, 1990). Further discussion of the validation studies on the SDLRS can be found in Brockett and Hiemstra (1991), Delahaye and Smith (1995), and Guglielmino (1997).

Research has suggested that individuals who have developed high self-directed learning skills tend to perform better in jobs requiring high degrees of problem-solving ability, creativity, and change.

Persons with low or below average SDLRS scores usually prefer very structured learning options, such as lectures in traditional classroom settings. Persons with average SDLRS scores are likely to be successful in some independent situations, but are not fully comfortable with handling the entire process of identifying their learning needs, planning their learning, and then implementing their learning plan. Persons with above average or high SDLRS scores usually prefer to determine their own learning needs, plan their learning, and then implement their learning plan. (This does not mean the persons with above average or high SDLRS scores never choose to be in a structured learning situation. They may choose traditional courses or workshops as a part of their learning plan.)

Appropriate Use of SDL

My second concern with Tough and Knowles' inspiring work involved the use of SDL without regard to the subject matter being learned. Certain business subjects (such as accounting), by nature, require the direction of a teacher/trainer. For example, the non-accountant does not know what he/she doesn't know or how to go about learning it.

To provide guidance for the appropriate use of SDL for different types of learning, I developed *The Continuum of Business Education* (Beitler, 2000; 2005, p.49). *The Continuum* recognizes the need of organizational members to acquire three types of skills: technical, people, and conceptual. These three types of skills are quite different in nature and require different teaching/learning strategies.

The Continuum of Business Education is helpful once the organizational members have demonstrated that they are ready to succeed at SDL. Lucy Guglielmino's SDLRS instrument is designed to indicate an individual's readiness to engage in SDL.

While knowing the individual's characteristics is critical for the successful use of SDL, two other variables must also be considered: the teacher characteristics and the subject matter/environmental characteristics. The SDL Variables Checklist (Beitler, 2001; 2005, p.50) provides a systematic way to consider the learner characteristics, the teacher characteristics, and the subject matter/environmental characteristics.

Learning Agreements

It is important not to think of self-directed versus teacher-directed education in terms of which one is better. There is not an ideal here; we must think in terms of which one is *appropriate*.

Is it possible for teacher-directed and self-directed learning to occur simultaneously in a single organization? Yes; in fact, both should be occurring simultaneously at all levels of the organization. Managing multiple teaching/learning processes throughout the organization can be facilitated by the use of learning agreements.

I have been a vocal advocate for the use of learning agreements (also called learning contracts) in organizations for many years (Beitler, 1999, 2000). But I didn't invent the concept.

Contract learning was advocated throughout the 1970s and 1980s by Knowles (1975, 1986). Knowles, who taught graduate students at Boston University and North Carolina State University, found lecturing to *older* students ineffective because of their unique backgrounds and needs. Knowles decided to write a learning contract with each of his students. The contract was an agreement between teacher and student; it detailed what would be learned and how it would be learned (Knowles, 1986).

Knowles' conception of the learning contract has been implemented in numerous graduate schools, including Norwich University (Montpelier, Vermont) and The Union Institute (Cincinnati, Ohio). Throughout the 1990s, I advocated the use of learning agreements with mid-career professionals and managers in organizational settings (Beitler, 1999, 2000).

While I have been an advocate of self-directed learning in organizations, I have always kept one of Knowles' warnings in mind. Knowles (1986) cautioned, "some people get so enamored of one technique that they use it in every situation, whether it is appropriate or not" (p.3). To heed his admonition, I have attempted to determine when self-directed learning is appropriate, and when it is not.

While I can argue for the use of both teacher-directed learning and self-directed learning in the organization (based on the SDL Variables Checklist), it is more important to discuss how to capture individual learning for the benefit of the entire organization. That is one of the major advantages of learning agreements. A learning agreement between the supervisor and his/her subordinate can incorporate teacher-directed and self-directed learning, as appropriate.

Learning agreements provide not only guidance for the individual manager; they provide a way to document, capture, and share knowledge throughout the organization. These agreements can provide the foundation for a learning organization in which individuals engage in self-directed study and then share their new knowledge with other organizational members.

Learning agreements are actually quite simple to write when they are incorporated into the performance evaluation process. The performance evaluation should include an analysis of the employee's learning and development needs.

Once the learning and development needs are agreed upon by the employee and his/her manager, only four writing steps are necessary (Beitler, 1999):

1. What will be learned?
2. How will it be learned?
3. How will the learning be documented?
4. How will the learning be evaluated?

The first step involves determining the learning objectives for the upcoming year. *What* will be learned must be determined (and agreed upon) before *how* it will be learned is considered.

The second step specifies the resources that will be used (for example, books, journal articles, workshops, mentoring, experiential learning, and so forth).

The third step defines how the learning will be documented (for example, through thematic papers, reaction papers, annotated bibliographies, videotapes, and so forth).

The fourth step defines how the learning will be evaluated, who will conduct the evaluation, and what the evaluation criteria are.

When incorporated into the annual performance appraisal process, learning agreements do not substantially increase the work on individual managers and workers. Learning agreements, utilizing both self-directed learning and teacher-directed learning, can dramatically improve an organization's ability to promote, reward, capture, and benefit from individual learning.

The documents generated by learning agreements become an essential part of the organization's knowledge management system. Let's look at knowledge management systems next.

Knowledge Management

It is critical for organizations to determine the essential knowledge needed for success. While a consultant can facilitate this process, it is necessary for senior management to be actively engaged in these discussions.

Once essential business knowledge has been identified, a knowledge management (KM) system can be designed to capture and transfer that essential knowledge. There are basically two different types of KM systems: codification and personalization.

Codification KM Systems

A codification KM system is appropriate for an organization that specializes in relatively "standardized" solutions for common problems. Codifiable knowledge is knowledge that can be easily articulated.

To some degree, every organization needs to codify knowledge. Where standardized processes and procedures exist, a codification KM system is appropriate.

Hansen, Nohria, and Tierney (2001) refer to the codification KM strategy as using a "people-to-document" approach (p.64). Codification KM systems separate the knowledge from the person who developed it. Once the knowledge has been extracted from the person, it is stored in an electronic database for subsequent retrieval and reuse by other organizational members, without any need for contacting the person who developed it. Therefore, this type of KM system is highly efficient for explicit (codifiable) knowledge.

The ultimate goal of the codification KM system is codify, store, and disseminate the knowledge that is critical in serving the needs of customers (as defined in the strategic plan).

Personalization KM Systems

A personalization KM system is appropriate for an organization that specializes in "customized" solutions for unique problems. Personalization KM systems focus on tacit knowledge. Tacit knowledge is knowledge that cannot be easily articulated.

While every organization needs to codify some knowledge, I believe it's the improvisations that make the expert a master (Beitler, 2005, p.65). This tacit knowledge, typically only shared between experts, creates what Ackerman (2000) calls the "social-technical gap."

Tacit knowledge stubbornly defies capture by codification systems. By its nature, tacit knowledge cannot be easily separated from the individual who created it. Since tacit knowledge is closely tied to its creator, a person-to-person approach (instead of the person-to-document approach of a codification system) must be utilized.

These person-to-person KM systems require large investments to create and support internal networks of experts. These systems only make financial sense when the strategic plan calls for customized solutions to unique problems for very substantial fees.

Documents in a personalization KM system serve the purpose of getting someone "up to speed." And then, higher-level tacit knowledge is transferred during face-to-face meetings.

If the organization requires a personalization KM system to capture and transfer tacit knowledge, one popular method is the community of practice. A community of practice is a group of peers who share a passion for a particular field of knowledge. They are informally bound and meet together face-to-face or electronically. While they may share books and other documents (codified knowledge), the primary focus of their meetings is the sharing of experiences and new ideas (tacit knowledge) that can be used in practice.

Primary/Secondary Systems

Determining a primary KM approach, codification or personalization, is a strategic decision. Senior management's clearly articulated competitive strategy should drive the determination of a primary KM strategy.

Hansen, et al. (2001) found, "Companies that use knowledge effectively pursue one strategy predominantly and use the second strategy to support the first. We think of this as an 80-20 split" (p.76). Organizations dividing resources equally between the two approaches, without being clear about what critical knowledge they need, invariably fail at both.

Corporate Universities

Obviously, every organization will not want to create a corporate university (CU). A CU requires the investment of substantial resources (time, energy, and money). But, every organization can benefit from knowing the strategies and practices of successful CUs.

Jeanne Meister, a leading authority on corporate universities, believes the CU can provide "The strategic umbrella for developing and educating employees, customers, and suppliers in order to meet an organization's business strategies" (1998, p.29).

CUs can provide learning opportunities for the company's entire value chain. An organization's value chain can include customers, suppliers, dealers, distributors, and even traditional educational institutions. The CU can be used as a relationship builder with the company's value chain members; ultimately, this can lead to a sustainable competitive advantage.

Every CU must be designed to support the organization's clearly defined mission and strategic plan. Therefore, every CU is (and should be) designed differently.

Designing a CU is a critical step. If the CU is not aligned with the organization's mission, or if it does not contribute to the implementation of the company's strategic plan, it does little more than generate large expenditures.

A corporate university should be seen as a strategy for establishing and maintaining a sustainable competitive advantage. But like any other sustainable competitive advantage, this strategy requires high-level support and leadership.

Summary

In this chapter, we have taken only a brief and cursory look at organizational learning and knowledge management interventions. But, I hope you can see the importance of these interventions in today's highly competitive, knowledge-driven organizations.

The concept of the learning organization, while inspiring, will remain only a concept unless appropriate OL/KM interventions are implemented to convert theory into practice. Every organization must promote, reward, and capture individual learning for the benefit of the organization. Every organization must continually create (or acquire), capture, and disseminate knowledge to remain competitive.

REFERENCES

Ackerman, M.S. (2000). The intellectual challenge of CSCW: The gap between social requirements and technical feasibility. *Human-Computer Interaction*, 15, 179-203.

Argyris, C. & Schön, D. (1976). *Organizational learning*. Reading, MA: Addison-Wesley.

Baskett, M. (1993). *Workplace factors that enhance self-directed learning*. (Text No. 93-01-002). Montreal, Canada: Group for Interdisciplinary Research on Autonomy and Training, University of Quebec at Montreal.

Beitler, M.A. (1999). Learning and development agreements with mid-career professionals. *Performance in Practice*, Fall 1999. American Society for Training & Development.

Beitler, M.A. (2000). Contract learning in organizational learning and management development. In H.B. Long and Associates (Eds.), *Practice and theory in self-directed learning*. Schaumberg, IL: Motorola University Press.

Beitler, M.A. (2001). Self-directed learning readiness at General Motors Japan. In H.B. Long and Associates (Eds.), *Expanding horizons in self-directed learning*. Schaumberg, IL: Motorola University Press.

Beitler, M.A. (2005). *Strategic organizational learning*. Greensboro, NC: Practitioner Press International.

Brockett, R. & Hiemstra, R. (1991). *Self-direction in adult learning: Perspectives on theory, research, and practice*. London: Routledge.

Confessore, S.J. & Kops, W.J. (1998). Self-directed learning and the learning organization: Examining the connection between the individual and the learning environment. *Human Resource Development Quarterly*, 9(4), pp.365-375.

Delahaye, B.L. & Smith, H.E. (1995). The validity of the Learning Preference Assessment. *Adult Education Quarterly*, 45(3), pp.159-173.

Dixon, N.M. (1994). Organizational learning: A review of the literature with implications for HRD professionals. *Human Resource Development Quarterly*, 3(1), pp.29-49.

Foucher, R. (1995). *Enhancing self-directed learning in the workplace: A model and a research agenda*. (Text No. 95-01-005). Montreal, Canada: Group for Interdisciplinary Research on Autonomy and Training, University of Quebec at Montreal.

Garrison, D.R. (1987). Self-directed and distance learning: Facilitating self-directed learning beyond the institutional setting. *International Journal of Lifelong Education*, 6(4), pp.309-318.

Guglielmino, L.M. (1978). Development of the Self-Directed Learning Readiness Scale (Doctoral dissertation, University of Georgia, 1977). *Dissertation Abstracts International*, 1978, 38, 6467A.

Guglielmino, L.M. (1997). Reliability and validity of the Self-Directed Learning Readiness Scale and the Learning Preference Assessment. In H.B. Long & Associates, *Expanding horizons in self-directed learning* (pp.209-222). Norman, OK: College of Education, University of Oklahoma.

Guglielmino, L.M. & Guglielmino, P.J. (1991a). *Expanding your readiness for self-directed learning: A workbook for the Learning Preference Assessment*. King of Prussia, PA: Organization Design and Development.

Guglielmino, L.M. & Guglielmino, P.J. (1991b). *Learning Preference Assessment facilitator guide*. King of Prussia, PA: Organization Design and Development.

Hansen, M., Nohria, N., & Tierney, T. (2001). What's your strategy for managing knowledge? Chapter in *Harvard Business Review on Organizational Learning*. Boston, MA: Harvard Business School Publishing.

Knowles, M. (1975). *Self-directed learning: A guide for learners and teachers*. Chicago: Follett.

Knowles, M. (1986). Using contract learning. San Francisco: Jossey-Bass.

Long, H.B. (1989). Truth unguessed and yet to be discovered: A professional's self-directed learning. In H.B. Long & Associates, *Self-directed learning: Emerging theory and practice* (pp.125-135). Norman, OK: Oklahoma Research Center for Continuing, Professional, and Higher Education of the University of Oklahoma.

Long, H.B. (1990). Psychological control in self-directed learning. *International Journal of Lifelong Education*, 9(4), 331-38.

Long, H.B. (1991). Challenges in the study and practice of self-directed learning. In H. B. Long & Associates, *Self-directed learning: Consensus and conflict* (pp.11-28). Norman, OK: Oklahoma Research Center for Continuing, Professional, and Higher Education of the University of Oklahoma.

Long, H.B. & Ageykum, S. (1988). Self-directed learning: Assessment and validation. In H.B. Long & Associates, *Self-directed learning: Application and theory* (pp.253-266). Athens, GA: Adult Education Department, University of Georgia.

Long, H.B. & Morris, S.(1995). Self-directed learning in business and industry: A review of the literature 1983-1993. In H.B. Long & Associates (Eds.), *New dimensions in self-directed learning*. Norman, OK: College of Education, University of Oklahoma.

McCune, S.K. (1989). A meta-analytic study of adult self-direction in learning: A review of the research from 1977 to 1987 (Doctoral dissertation, Texas A&M University, 1988). *Dissertation Abstracts International*, 1989, 49, 3237.

McCune, S.K., Guglielmino, L.M., & Garcia, G. (1990). Adult self-direction in learning: A preliminary meta-analytic investigation of research using the Self-Directed Learning Readiness Scale. In H.B. Long & Associates, *Advances in self-directed learning research* (pp.145-156). Norman, OK: Oklahoma Research Center for Continuing, Professional, and Higher Education of the University of Oklahoma.

Meister, J. (1998). *Corporate universities*, (rev. ed.). New York: McGraw-Hill.

Merriam, S. & Brockett, R. (1997). *The profession and practice of adult education*. San Francisco: Jossey-Bass.

Senge, P.M. (1990). *The fifth discipline: The art and practice of the learning organization*. New York: Doubleday.

Tough, A. (1979). *The adult's learning projects* (2nd ed.). Toronto: Ontario Institute for Studies in Education.

CHAPTER 13

Evaluating OC

The last step in the Action Research Model (step 6) is **evaluation**. Unfortunately, this step rarely gets the attention it deserves. There are two separate, but related, things to evaluate. First, we will examine the issues involved in evaluating the OC intervention itself. Then, we will look at the complex issues involved in evaluating the OC consultant.

Evaluation of the OC Intervention

The evaluation of an OC intervention leads to two possible conclusions: positive or negative.

Hopefully, positive changes (resulting from our OC interventions) can be institutionalized. Institutionalization involves making these changes an on-going part of the organization's regular operations.

Increasingly, senior management will be demanding justification for expenditures on all corporate projects, including OC projects. As globalization and technological advances increase competitive pressures on organizations, all successful organizations will have to control their costs. OC consultants don't have to become cost accountants, but they must be able to communicate their understanding of the bottomline perspective.

It is essential that evaluation criteria be established early in the action research process. Objectives and possible outcomes must be realistic. It's a big mistake to allow the client members to maintain unrealistic expectations until the end of the OC process. Discuss expectations early and often!

Two Types of Evaluation for OC Interventions

When evaluating OC interventions, it is important to conduct both

process evaluation and **outcome evaluation**. There is a tendency to evaluate only the outcomes of OC interventions, partly due to the typical senior management preoccupation with outcomes. Nevertheless, OC consultants should also insist on process evaluation. Let's look first at process evaluation.

Process evaluation involves *how* interventions are implemented. I stated earlier that proper diagnosis is essential before attempting to choose an intervention(s). It is equally important to implement the intervention(s) properly. Choosing the proper intervention(s) must be followed by proper implementation of those planned interventions.

Process evaluation can be conducted **during** as well as **after** implementation. Some interventions lend themselves easily to periodic process evaluation. For example, at three-day interventions, I frequently use "check-outs" and "check-ins." Check-outs are round-robin discussions at the end of the day that review lessons learned, frustrations, and other concerns. Check-ins are conducted at the beginning of each day. They allow for reflection on the earlier day(s), after "sleeping on it." Check-outs and check-ins give the OC consultant opportunities to make changes *during* the intervention.

Process evaluation is also important *after* implementation. Did the intervention go as planned? Perhaps the proper intervention was chosen, but it was poorly implemented.

Now, let's turn our attention to outcome evaluation. Outcome evaluation is concerned with "the overall impact of the intervention, and with whether resources should continue to be allocated to it or to other possible interventions" (Cummings & Worley, 2001, p.176).

Cummings and Worley (2001) view negative results this way: "Negative results on these measures tell members (and OC consultants) that the initial diagnosis was flawed or that the wrong intervention was chosen. Such feedback might prompt additional diagnosis and a search for a more effective intervention" (p.176). Negative results may call for another iteration of the Action Research Model, beginning with additional data gathering.

Positive results of outcome evaluation should lead to discussion about institutionalizing the changes. We will discuss institutionalization later in this chapter.

Outcome evaluation attempts to measure changes in:

1. productivity
2. job satisfaction
3. absenteeism or turnover
4. quality
5. organizational climate

Senior management invariably looks for these types of results. The OC consultant should expect to be asked to discuss these results with senior management members.

Designing Evaluation Measurements

Discussions concerning the design of evaluation measurements can quickly become extremely technical. While OC practitioners should know the basics of operational definitions, reliability, validity, and research design, the more technical arguments should be left to the academic researchers.

For the practitioner, the concept of "operational definition" is an important issue. In practice, the OC consultant should spend time collaboratively developing operational definitions with the client. There should be agreement on these definitions. Cummings and Worley (2001) believe a good measure is operationally defined when "it specifies the empirical data needed, how they will be collected and, most important, how they will be converted from data to information" (p.180).

Reliability is concerned with the accuracy of the measurement. Every measurement can be accused of a bias. For this reason, I recommend using multiple measures (questionnaires, interviews, among others). If the independent measurements agree, reliability is increased.

Reliability can be enhanced by using standardized instruments that have been subjected to reliability and validity testing. Two organizations can be contacted for more information about these instruments: the Institute for Social Research at the University of Michigan (www. isr.umich.edu) and the Center for Effective Organizations at the University of Southern California (www.marshall.usc.edu/ceo).

A valid measurement measures what it claims to measure. A method of measurement may be valid for one variable and invalid for another.

Textbooks discuss content validity and face validity. Content validity is determined by "experts," but in practice, face validity is critical. Clients lose confidence in consultants when measurements don't "look valid."

Finally, we should keep in mind that quasi-experimental research designs are used in assessing OC interventions. Quasi-experimental research designs have inherent problems. "These designs are not as rigorous and controlled as are randomized experimental designs" (Cummings & Worley, 2001, p.184). Even with these limitations, these methods are still valuable tools. Cummings and Worley (2001) sum up the value of these tools by saying, "they allow evaluations to rule out many rival explanations for OC results other than the intervention itself" (p.184).

Institutionalizing OC

Discussions about institutionalization usually take place in a positive atmosphere. These discussions begin after an OC intervention has resulted in positive change. You may recall the section in chapter two on Lewin's Three Stage Model of Change, where Lewin spoke of unfreezing, moving, and refreezing. Institutionalization is what Lewin would call refreezing.

Ideally, these new changes will no longer require the monitoring of a manager or change agent; the changes now become part of the organizational culture.

A distinction should be made here between evolutionary and revolutionary change. With evolutionary change, for example TQM (total quality management), it is the philosophy **not** a fixed result or procedure that will be institutionalized (frozen). Obviously, in TQM we want continuous improvement. We don't want to freeze the production defects at a certain level. We want to freeze (institutionalize) the TQM philosophy.

With revolutionary change, e.g., conflict resolution, it may be desirable to institutionalize the change. For example, if two highly interdependent departments were not working well together before, but now they are, we want to make that permanent. Institutionalizing the change may involve changing reward systems, workflows, reporting hierarchies, and other processes.

Goodman and Dean (1982) have developed a model for the institutionalization process. They believe there are three key **organizational characteristics** affecting the institutionalization of organizational changes: congruence, stability of environment and technology, and unionization. Congruence is the degree of "harmony with the organization's managerial philosophy, strategy, and structure; its current environment; and other changes taking place" (Cummings & Worley, 2001). When the changes are perceived to be congruent with these dimensions, the likelihood of institutionalization is increased. The opposite is also true, if the perceived degree of congruence is low, the likelihood of institutionalization is low.

The roles of stability of environment and technology, and unionization, in Goodman and Dean's (1982) model are rather obvious. Instability in the environment, including changes in technology, brings with it forces for change, not stability. Unions, which are more influential in Europe than in the U.S., can be powerful forces for or against change.

Goodman and Dean (1982) believe the following five **OC intervention characteristics** will improve the institutionalization process:

1. goal specificity — intervention goals should clearly link rewards and new behaviors

2. programmability — intervention characteristics should be specified clearly in advance

3. level of change target — many targets for organizational change are susceptible to countervailing forces from other parts of the

organization

4. internal support — institutionalization requires the support of internal change agents (external consultants are only a temporary part of the typical client organization)

5. sponsorship — change requires a powerful sponsor or champion (the sponsor must be high enough in the organization to control essential resources)

Goodman and Dean (1982) also list five **institutionalization processes/implementation characteristics** that will affect the successful "refreezing" of change:

1. socialization — implementing change involves new learning (new behaviors, norms, and values must be transferred through the training or re-training of organizational members)

2. commitment — people should be able to select the new behaviors freely and publicly

3. reward allocation — rewards must be available to reinforce desired behaviors. Rewards, both intrinsic and extrinsic, must be linked to the new desired behaviors

4. diffusion — all changes will face resistance. A change must have the ability to spread throughout the organization, even against counter norms and values

5. sensing and calibration — this requires detecting deviations from desired behaviors, and then taking corrective actions

The last part of Goodman and Dean's (1982) model looks at the **indicators of institutionalization.** "Institutionalization is not an all-or-nothing concept," say Cummings and Worley (2001, p.192). The following five questions indicate the degree of institutionalization:

1. Knowledge — Do members have enough knowledge to perform the new behaviors?

2. Performance — What percentage of organizational members are actually performing the new behaviors?

3. Preferences — Have the new behaviors become personal preferences for individual members?

4. Normative consensus — Do organizational members agree about the appropriateness of the changes?

5. Value consensus — Is the consensus about the values that support the new behaviors?

Evaluating the Consultant

This a good place to discuss the issues involved in evaluating the consultant. The best work in this area is Alfred Kieser's of the University of Mannheim (Germany). Kieser is often critical of consultants. What he describes as "management consulting fads" and "applying theories of fashion to management consulting" (Kieser, 2002; Ernst & Kieser, 2002) are detrimental to the client company. OC consultants who follow Schein's Process Consulting Model, including the underlying motivation of "being helpful," should guide the client around these "management fads" and "management fashions."

Kieser (2002) sees management scientists (university professors), management consultants, and managers operating in three different systems. He believes these three "social systems" pursue "different goals," and develop "their own rationalities" and "rhetoric."

Kieser's (2002) work challenges the widely held assumption (for example, Nohria & Eccles, 1998) that knowledge passes from management scientists through management consultants to business managers. This traditional belief that consultants are "agents for the transfer of best practices" (March, 1991), or disseminators of management science, is critically examined by Kieser.

To create a better dialog between management scientists, management consultants, and business managers, it is important to be aware of the systems in which each of the three operates. Let's begin by looking at the world of management scientists.

The World of Management Scientists

Management science is a subsystem of the system of science (Kieser, 2002). University professor/researchers proudly describe themselves as scientists. As members of the scientific community, they conform to the norms and rules of that community. The scientific community determines what kinds of information belong to science and what kinds do not (Krough & Roos, 1995).

Kieser (2002) lists the following additional determinations made by the scientific community (the system):

1. which sets of statements qualify as a theory
2. which criteria empirical tests of hypotheses must meet
3. which research methods are acceptable
4. what qualifies as data
5. what qualifies as a scientific finding

It is important to understand that scientists operate within this system. Knowledge created by the system is limited by the boundaries established by the system.

Production within the scientific community is represented by published articles in scientific journals. Scientific journals are written by scientists for scientists. When universities evaluate professors, publications that target practitioners "do not count as an indicator of scientific achievement" (Kieser, 2002).

Management scientists, like other scientists, acquire their reputations in several ways (Kieser, 2002):

1. getting their manuscripts published in scientific journals
2. being cited by other scientists
3. getting job offers from prestigious universities
4. receiving research grants
5. receiving scientific rewards

Kieser (2002) believes the scientific community has erected communication barriers to demarcate the borders of science. The rhetoric typically involves difficult mathematical models and complex statistical analyses. Scientific argumentation must be impersonal and skeptical of its own results.

The contrast between the scientist and consultant should be clearly understood by the business manager. The nature of the scientist's work makes problems more complex, while the consultant's work attempts to simplify problems (more about the consultant in a moment).

Scientists work to extend and refine existing theories, leading to more complexity. Even the scientist's research methods become more complex as the methods get more refined. It is not realistic for consultants and business managers to look to management scientists for simplistic applications of scientific theories to management practice.

The worlds of consultants and managers are dramatically different from the world of the scientist. Now, let's look at the world of the consultant.

The World of Management Consultants

Kieser (2002) reminds us that the activities of the consultant "are not keyed to the criterion true/false, but to the criterion profitable/not profitable." Consulting profits come from reformulating complex problems so that they appear simple for the ultimate decision maker. As stated earlier, "theories normally tend to make decisions more complicated" (Kieser, 2002).

Consultants reframe management problems that are perceived as unstructured into structured ones on the basis of simple pragmatic assumptions. Consulting solutions typically appeal to a manager's common sense, not to scientific proofs. The goal of the consultant's work is to simplify.

The simplification work of consultants usually involves the use of catchy labels, checklists, lists of steps (procedures), matrices, and other devices. Visual simplicity is especially important when **selling** an idea to the management team.

For example, one popular bit of consulting advice is as follows:

Have producers of internal services justify their activities, and internal customers justify their need. Then eliminate those services that are least valuable to the organization.

This is common sense. No scientific proof is offered by the consultant; no scientific proof is requested by management. The client will be satisfied (and will pay), if it works. Proof of its working is accomplished with a variety of pragmatic measures, such as *Were costs reduced?*, *Is employee attendance higher?*.

Ernst and Kieser (2002) list several "unofficial" functions of consultants:

1. legitimization — a consultant signals to major stakeholders that "best practices" are being applied

2. weapons of politics — consultants are instrumental in increasing the power of groups of managers

3. fostering careers of sponsors — consultants always try to put their sponsors in the most favorable light

4. neutral discussion partner — consultants can be a sounding board for ideas and strategies

Consulting is a business. For a consulting firm to operate efficiently (more profitably) it may consider the process of "commodifying" or packaging solutions. Ernst and Kieser (2002) see several reasons why consulting firms would do this:

1. greater potential for attracting clients — packaged approaches appear tested and proven

2. greater potential for marketing — catchy labels (e.g., Zero-Based Budgeting) stimulate dialog (and interest) in potential client organizations

3. facilitation of coordination within the consulting firm — consultants within the firm "work with the same schemas and instruments"

4. less experienced consultants can replace more experienced consultants by following highly structured processes

Consultants offer "ideas, metaphors, models, and words that impose order on a confusing world" (March, 1991, p.29). Packaged, simple solutions are very appealing to overworked business managers.

Kieser has written extensively about how consultants use rhetoric to create "management fashions" (Kieser, 1997, 2002; Ernst & Kieser, 2002). He believes the process of establishing management fashions (or fads) follows this pattern:

1. a discourse develops around a buzzword (i.e. Lean Production or Reengineering)
2. the discourse is triggered by and produced in many different forms (texts) — books, articles, speeches, workshops, internet forums, etc.
3. several texts on new management concepts compete simultaneously
4. texts with the most rhetorical quality (see Furusten, 1998) and timeliness (see Abrahamson, 1996) attract management attention
5. if management attention grows wide enough, a management fashion is born.

Ernst and Kieser (2002) state, "In the majority of cases consultants are the originators of texts of this sort. Usually the texts contain a number of expressions or principles that are vague like empowerment, internal customers, or process ownership. Vagueness is a strength since it triggers discussions…and increases the desire to learn more"(p.14).

"Management fashions" are often "supported" by university professors, publishers, editors of management magazines, and commercial seminar organizers, as they attempt to keep up with new management concepts.

The World of Managers

The business manager is expected to keep things under control. Achieving control is one of the strongest human motives (Adler, 1929). Consequently, the perception of a loss of control leads to intense efforts to regain control (Thompson, 1981). Today's manager is "confronted with the perception of an increasingly complex and dynamic inner and outer organizational environment. The sheer presence of experts is often sufficient to heighten a manager's perception of controllability" (Ernst & Kieser, 2002).

By copying the new practices being implemented by the competition, "managers get the impression that they are on the right track" (Ernst & Kieser, 2002). Many managers will buy the new consulting solutions simply to be sure they don't fall behind the competition. The risk appears minimal since failure of the solution puts the organization in no worse a situation than the competition. Fear of being left behind is a powerful motivator to buy the consultant's solution.

So what's a manager to do? The management scientist appears to overcomplicate; the management consultant appears to oversimplify. I believe today's business manager can benefit from the knowledge generated by both of these systems. But to do so, the manager must be aware of the strengths and limitations of each system.

Many problems in management practice require only pragmatic solutions, not scientific explanations. The strength of the consulting system is its ability to produce these pragmatic solutions. The limitation of the consulting system is its self-serving profit orientation. Managers certainly can benefit from the consultant's pragmatic solutions but must be aware of the consultant's tendency to sell packaged solutions.

Management scientists also have something to offer to business managers. The scientist's system detaches emotionality from the decision-making process. The rationality and logic of a decision can be enhanced by the scientist's theory and research. The scientific approach is often time-consuming, but can be extremely valuable in a multimillion dollar decision.

The Problems with Evaluation

"Management theorists are yet to come to an agreement on the question of how any organizational decision can be judged in terms of its effectiveness" (Ernst & Kieser, 2002). Unclear or conflicting goals, complex causality relations, and uncertain long-term plans are some of the problems with evaluating effectiveness (Lewin & Minton, 1986; March & Sutton, 1997).

Organizational change consulting is a knowledge-intensive professional service. Various aspects of the nature of the service (the difference in qualification between consultant and client; their interaction during service delivery, as well as the intangibility, singularity, and indeterminability of outcomes) are responsible for the evaluation difficulties (Ernst & Kieser, 2002).

There are two major problems when managers attempt to evaluate

OC interventions and consultants. First, the manager does not know what would have happened if he or she had acted otherwise. Second, the manager must attempt "to assess whether the consultant is really knowledgeable or only knows how to manage impressions" (Ernst & Kieser, 2002).

According to agency theory (Eisenhardt, 1989), significant knowledge asymmetry exists between the consultant (agent) and the client (principal). Managers typically feel somewhat dependent on consultants to define the organization's problems and to recommend solutions. Naturally, there is a tendency for consultants to find organizational problems that fit the solutions they offer.

As stated back in Chapter 3, Schein's Process Consulting Model sees OC efforts as a collaborative process involving both consultant and client. The social nature of the working relationship has implications for the outcomes of the OC effort. Invariably, the responsibility for success or failure becomes blurred. When the client attempts to evaluate the consultant's performance, he or she encounters the problem of not being able to separate his own contributions from the consultant's. "The evaluation of the consulting project becomes highly subjective" (Ernst & Kieser, 2002). "In the absence of reliable and accessible evaluation criteria, the perceived quality of the relationship often becomes a dominant factor in pre- and post-purchase evaluation" (Clark, 1995).

Clark (1995) clearly states, "No consulting project can be reproduced in an identical manner." This reality makes evaluation highly unscientific. "The client has no possibility to compare the performance of consultants contracted by him to any other case which might deliver indications for possible evaluation criteria" (Ernst & Kieser, 2002).

Ernst and Kieser (2002) also point out the indeterminable or uncontrollable aspects of the consultant's efforts. They believe consulting "has an effect on a large number of variables throughout the client organization. To a certain extent, this impact cannot be controlled."

One final issue concerns timing of the effects. Immediately after completion of the intervention, typically when evaluation is done, "the client will have difficulties in assessing whether and when the intended (or unintended) impact will show" (Ernst & Kieser, 2002).

Conclusion

Evaluation cannot be based on clearly objective criteria or scientific findings. The judgement of success (or failure) of an OC intervention and the effectiveness (or ineffectiveness) of an OC consultant, are largely based on the perceptions and expectations of the client and consultant involved in the OC effort. This fact emphasizes the importance of an on-going dialog between client and consultant about perceptions and expectations. As stated in this chapter, the manager and consultant are in two different worlds. Only open and honest communication can bridge the gap between these two worlds.

REFERENCES

Abrahamson, E. (1996). Management fashion. *Academy of Management Review*, 21, pp.254-285.

Adler, A. (1929). *The science of living*. New York: Greenberg.

Clark, T. (1995). *Managing consultants: Consultancy as the management of impressions*. Buckingham, England: Open University Press.

Cummings, T.G. & Worley, C.G. (2001). *Organization development and change* (7th ed.). Cincinnati, OH: South-Western.

Eisenhardt, K. (1989). Agency theory: An assessment and review. *Academy of Management Review*, 14, pp.57-77.

Ernst, B. & Kieser, A. (2002) In search of explanations for the consulting explosion. In L. Engwall & K. Sahlin-Andersson (Eds.), *The expansion of management knowledge: carriers, ideas, and circulation*. Stanford, CA: Stanford University Press.

Furusten, S. (1998). The creation of popular management texts. In J.L. Alvarez (Ed.), *The diffusion and consumption of business knowledge* (pp.141-163). London: McMillan.

Goodman, P. & Dean, J. (1982). Creating long-term organizational change. In P. Goodman (Ed.), *Change in organization*, (pp.226-79). San Francisco: Jossey-Bass.

Kieser, A. (1997). Myth and rhetoric in management fashion. *Organization*, 4 (1), 49-74.

Kieser, A. (2002). On communication barriers between management science, consultancies, and business organizations. In T. Clark & R. Fincham (Eds.), *Critical consulting: New perspectives on the management advice industry*. Oxford, UK: Blackwell Publishers.

Lewin, A.Y. & Minton, J.W. (1986). Determining organizational effectiveness: Another look, and an agenda for research. *Management Science*, 32, pp.514-538.

March, J.G. (1991). Organizational consultants and organizational research. *Journal of Applied Communication Research*, 19, 20-31.

March, J.G. & Sutton, R.I. (1997). Organizational performance as a dependent variable. *Organization Science*, 8 (6), pp.698-706.

Nohria, N. & Eccles, R. (1998). Where does management knowledge come from? In J.L. Alvarez (Ed.), *The diffusion and consumption of business knowledge*, pp.278-304. London: McMillan.

Thompson, S.C. (1981). Will it hurt less if I can control it? A complex answer to a simple question. *Psychological Bulletin*, 90, 89-101.

Von Krogh, G. & Roos, J. (1995). *Organizational epistemology*. London: Mcmillan.

CHAPTER 14

The Future of OC

In his thought-provoking book, *The Singularity is Near* (Kurzweil, 2006), inventor, futurist, and MIT professor Ray Kurzweil predicts a coming period of exponential change that human brains will not be able to handle without help. The "help" will come in the form of technology (such as computer chips) being implanted in our heads to give us the processing speed we'll need to keep up with the rate of change.

Even if you believe Kurzweil's predictions are too extreme, all of us would agree that the rate of change will continue to accelerate. How we handle the challenge of an accelerating rate of change will become a critical issue for organizational success in the future. Almost everything we currently do in organizations will change.

I want to look at a few particular areas where we'll see dramatic change.

21st Century Organizations

For many years, we all heard predictions of intellectual assets becoming more important to organizations than tangible assets. We are now well into an era of intellectual assets. "Capital spending on information technology, which in 1965 was only one-third of that of production technology, now exceeds it" (Stewart, 1997).

Information technology will allow organizations to maintain large databases of customer needs and preferences. The new customer-based operations will cause organizations to move away from traditional hierarchies toward inter-company collaborative ventures. These new structures will include suppliers, customers, and even old competitors.

Before the turn of the century, Dunning (1999) described three stages of market-based capitalism based on three key characteristics:

1) 17th and 18th Centuries:
   primary source of wealth — land
   spatial dimension — local
   organizational form — feudal or entrepreneurial

2) 19th and 20th Centuries:
   primary source of wealth — machines
   spatial dimension — regional/national
   organizational form — corporate hierarchy

3) 21st Century:
   primary source of wealth — knowledge
   spatial dimension — global
   organizational form — alliances

Dunning (1999) believed these changes are the causes for the reconfiguration of value-added activities, the expansion of spatial dimensions, and the restructuring of organizational forms. These changes will result in "soft boundaries" for organizations (p.6).

While large corporations are downsizing the value-added activities they do in-house, "they are not replacing these with arm's length transactions, but rather with a series of on-going and hands-on technological and marketing relationships with their new suppliers, customers, and competitors" (Dunning, 1999, p.6).

Dunning (1999, p.7) offers the following comparisons of the old and new paradigms:

Old — an organizer of human and physical resources
New — an innovator and product improver

Old — gain competitive advantage with tangible assets
New — gain competitive advantage with core competencies

Old — "an island of conscious power"
New — a member of an alliance or network

Old — arm's length relationships with suppliers and customers
New — partnerships with suppliers and customers

The network structures of the 21st century will afford distinct advantages. Network structures will enable organizations "to gain many of the efficiencies traditionally reserved for large firms while remaining small and nimble" (Cummings & Worley, 2008, p.617). Network structures can quickly adapt to changing customer needs.

21st Century Workforce *5 characteristics*

Walter Oechsler of the University of Mannheim (Germany) believes the workplace and workforce in the 21st century will be characterized by "flexibilization." Oechsler (2000) sees the "flexibilization" of the workplace and workforce leading to "a core group with unlimited full employment, and an increasingly larger group of short-term limited and/or part-time employees who face severe employment risks, ultimately resulting in stress."

I must agree with Oechsler's rather unpleasant prediction. Increasing global competition will lead to increasing pressure and stress on all employees. Employees who are unprepared for the new workplace will find themselves at great risk.

Oechsler (2000) goes on to describe a major change in corporate strategy. "Whereas the typical corporate strategy of the industrial society was uniform mass production with Tayloristic structures and stable employment, the dominant strategy for global competition is flexible specialization...The strategy of flexible specialization is directed toward customer needs" (Oechsler, 2000).

This shift in focus from fixed standardized production schedules to flexible customized customer services will dramatically affect the workplace and workforce. The 21st-century employee will have to bring a "flexible specialization" (Oechsler, 2000) to the 21st-century organization.

Twenty-first century organizations will only be interested in hiring employees who bring a specialization that will serve the flexible needs of customer/clients. Staff positions to support these customer-driven processes will still be available, but these staff positions (non-core competencies) will constantly be re-evaluated in light of possible outsourcing.

Employee loyalty will continue to decrease. Except for a small group of core professionals, employees will have to adopt a mindset of "selling their special competencies to different employers" (Oechsler, 2000). Oechsler (2000) envisions these employees as "entrepreneurs marketing their own human resources in order to make a living" (p.29). Employability will be the key to employee survival, not the stability of the company.

Another powerful trend in the workplace will be the technologically possible "virtual company." Oechsler (2000) believes the virtual company can suppress social interaction and lead to new forms of alienation. What we know about group dynamics in face-to-face interactions will have to be re-examined in virtual interactions. How will employees react in the decentralized work structures of the virtual companies?

Oechsler (2000) believes, "Information technologies will dissolve social entities" (p.28). If Oechsler is correct, what new entities and relationships will be created? I assume the social aspect of our human nature hasn't changed. Will this lead more individuals to social media?

Oechsler (2000) summarizes his predictions for the 21st century workforce by saying, "The employee will take on more and severe risks of being unemployed" (p.31). He is certainly right about that.

The work of OC consultants will be dramatically affected by these changes in employer-employee relations. The downsizing, outsourcing, and global alliances that began to grab headlines in the 1980s were not simply fads driven by a few "greedy capitalists." These trends are indicators of the more powerful megatrends of increasing global competition and increasing technological sophistication. No doubt, numerous psychosocial problems will arise from these trends.

OC & Globalization

The on-going globalization of business will continue to have profound effects on both the practice of management and the practice of OC. Managers and OC consultants must be aware of the implications of the globalization of business on the practice of their professions.

Globalization does not mean the "Microsoft-ization," or "American-ization," or "GE-ization" of business practice. Successful globalization of business practice will involve the blending of international cultures. This means managers and OC consultants must understand cultural differences, and be willing to compromise on a variety of practices.

Oechsler's Research

Some of the cultural differences between various cultures have become formalized as laws. Employee relations are regulated by national and/or local governments.

Walter Oechsler of the University of Mannheim (Germany) has provided insight into the duality of the globalization of business and the localization (nationalization) of employment relations (Oechsler, 1999). Oechsler states, "Globalization was enhanced by the liberalization of world markets and the almost free movement of capital throughout the world. At the same time, national governments... still regulate their national and local employment relations" (1999, p.97).

Oechsler (1999, p.97) asks this question, "How does global management cope with local employment relations?" His question is important for all change agents. Change involving employees (virtually all change efforts) must be determined and implemented in light of the prevailing political forces in each country where change is necessary.

While European countries are struggling to reconcile their economic differences, dramatic differences in employee relations still exist from one EU country to another. OC efforts involving more than one country (European or anywhere else) must be adjusted for these differences. Oechsler's (1999) work reminds us that national regulations will affect OC efforts involving the following:

employee participation

collective bargaining

social security/job security

working hours

working conditions

dismissals

retraining

flexibility of employment

In addition to Oechsler's (1999) work on the legal constraints on OC efforts, Hofstede's (2001, 1993) and Trompenaars' (2011) work on differences in cultural expectations must also be considered by change agents during international change efforts.

The Role of the Expatriate Manager

Most OC efforts in global business organizations are, by necessity, the responsibility of expatriate managers. Expatriate managers are managers working in countries other than their home countries. Successful implementation of OC efforts in these global businesses will require expatriate managers with cross-cultural management skills.

While the topic of training and support for expatriate managers is beyond the scope of this book, it's critical that we appreciate the importance of an organization's expatriate workers. For a more detailed discussion of expatriate training, see Beitler, 2010, Chapter 7.

Expatriate managers, especially U.S. managers working in foreign countries, experience very high failure rates. Black and Gregersen (1999) reported the following alarming findings:

1. Nearly one-third of U.S. managers sent abroad do not perform up to the expectations of their superiors.

2. Up to 20 percent of all U.S. managers sent abroad return early because of job dissatisfaction or difficulties in adjusting to a foreign country.

3. One-fourth of U.S. managers completing a foreign assignment left their company within one year after repatriation (often joining a competitor).

Perhaps, what is even more disturbing than Black and Gregersen's findings is the fact that we have known about these appalling failure rates for many years. In January of 1990, a *Training & Development*

Journal article stated, "Up to 40 percent of U.S. expatriate managers fail in their overseas assignments" (Hogan and Goodson, 1990).

The costs of these expatriate management failures are very high for the managers and their companies. Managers report personal relationship problems with family members who move to the foreign country with them, and a sense of disconnect with their families and friends in their home countries. Managers also report a fear of career derailment resulting from foreign assignment failure.

The companies experience very high costs when their expatriates fail, in terms of opportunity costs and hard costs. Opportunity costs include the loss of future business and reputation in the country. The failure of a U.S. manager enforces the stereotype of the culturally inept American.

Hard costs of these failures for U.S. companies are staggering. One American expatriate manager I interviewed reported receiving a $10,000 per month housing allowance from her multinational corporation while on a two-year assignment in Tokyo. She personally added a $1,000 per month to the allowance to rent an apartment. Add the cost of several trips home per year, and multiply that by several hundred expatriate managers and one gets an idea of the hard costs involved.

OC and IT

Without any doubt, I can predict the continuation of the megatrend of increasing application of information technology (IT). In the years ahead, IT will have an on-going and profound effect on all aspects of business and management. Thus, OC consultants and change agents must be aware of new developments and applications of IT. Expect every aspect of practice to be affected by IT.

In chapter 9, we discussed Schein's (2010) work on the influence of IT culture on organizational culture. Schein (2010) sees IT as a subculture of the organization. He believes subcultures can be completely congruent, supportive, stand in opposition to, or independent of the organization (2010, p.277). The implications of Schein's statement are obvious. We want the IT subculture to be supportive of (completely congruent with, if possible) the organization's strategy, structure, culture, and processes.

Schein (2010) and others (Van Maanen & Barley, 1984; Orlikowsli, 1988) describe IT as an "occupational community." An occupational community is a "group of practitioners, researchers, and teachers who have a common base of knowledge, a common jargon, similar background and training, and a sense of identifying with each other" (Schein, 2010, p.278). Schein (2010) goes on to say that an occupational community has a "shared set of basic assumptions about itself, its work, its relationship to its environment, and its clients" (p.278). These characteristics help explain the similarities in thinking and assumptions between IT teachers, IT consultants, and IT organizational members.

These shared assumptions in the IT occupational community often differ from the shared assumptions of general managers. These differences can lead to difficulties in implementing IT-related OC efforts. Managers and OC consultants should be aware of the basic IT assumptions.

The following discussion about the differences in assumptions between the IT occupational community and senior managers is admittedly oversimplified. Nevertheless, the differences must be considered when attempting to implement IT-dependent OC efforts.

Today, very few senior managers could be classified as "nonusers" of IT, unlike the scenario of the 1990s. However, many senior managers today are still under-utilizers of IT. Much of the resistance of senior managers to IT concerns the type of information, its packaging, and its transmission. Unlike IT professionals, many general managers prefer a more holistic, dynamic, face-to-face interaction that they believe is lacking in IT systems. Managers often see IT data as only raw data devoid of emotion and intuition.

General managers, I have spoken with, often admit to being "stressed-out," even humiliated, when trying to learn new IT applications. The cognitive style involved in communicating with desktop terminals is totally alien to some general mangers.

In Schein's (2010) study of how general managers view the IT community, he found the following beliefs about IT professionals:

1. oriented toward discovering optimal or final solutions

2. intolerant of ambiguity

3. little sympathy for "satisficing"

4. oriented toward clear rules and procedures

5. concrete and oriented toward quick feedback

6. task oriented more than people oriented

7. long-range oriented

8. decisive in decision making

9. control oriented (attempt to eliminate human error and "irrationality")

10. more interested in hardware and systems than people problems

General managers see some of these traits as positive and others as negative. General managers also express the concern that IT professions write instructions "for people like themselves" (Schein, 2010, p.283).

Zuboff (1988) offered some insight into the assumptions general managers make about their jobs. She believes that, historically, the rationalized and routinized work should be delegated to lower levels. The job of senior managers involves intuition, judgment, wisdom, and experience. IT forces more "rational" decisions. Zuboff's (1988) insight helps to explain some of the IT resistance of senior managers.

Another concern about IT is that large amounts of data will lead to managers' "micromanaging" or "overmanaging." Micromanaging leads to several dysfunctional consequences. First, lower level managers fail to develop. Second, self-management and self-control decreases. Third, intuition and experience are devalued in the decision-making process. Fourth, senior managers become overly concerned with details and lose sight of the big picture.

An essential key to understanding the resistance of general managers to IT-related change is a psychological approach. Managers will resist if they believe the IT change will make their position vulnerable.

The OC consultant must be aware of the assumptions (including fears) of the IT practitioners and the general managers. Assumptions based on fears can derail the OC effort.

21st Century OC Practice

The issues we have discussed in this chapter (flexibilization, globalization and localization, the widespread new uses of IT, and the new structures of organizations themselves) will have profound effects on the work of OC consultants, both internal and external.

OC is still a new profession. Internal and external practitioners will have to work to develop credibility and professionalism.

Internal OC consultants will have to work to gain full acceptance as strategic partners on senior management teams. To be accepted in that high-level role, they must bring high levels of value to the organization. In the 21st century, internal OC consultants will have to possess expertise in business strategy, organizational design, organizational culture, and organizational learning, in addition to the group dynamics expertise possessed by their 20th century counterparts.

External OC consultants must also work toward professionalizing their practice. Since OC is not a regulated profession, there is no oversight of OC consultants. While I would oppose government regulation, the ease of entry into OC practice is a problem. Anybody can hang out a shingle with the self-proclamation — OC Consultant. This has led to some embarrassing OC practice. Like any other profession, the OC profession must create a way to police itself.

As I stated earlier, OC theory and practice must become a part of senior management strategic planning. Cummings and Worley (2008) believe, "When managers integrate [OC knowledge] into their role, change capabilities will be diffused throughout the organization rather than located in a special function or role" (p.618). They go on to say, the "interventions themselves will be integrated into core business processes" (p.619).

Organizational change consultants will need to continuously update their knowledge of the new technological tools (such as groupware). As client organizations grow globally, they will need asynchronous as well as synchronous communication. These styles of communication will dramatically affect our understanding of group dynamics. "Processes of visioning, diagnosis, data feedback, and action planning will have to be reengineered to leverage new technologies" (Cummings & Worley, 2008, p.619).

Cummings and Worley (2008) believe "cycle times will be shorter" (p.620). OC consultants must take advantage of any opportunities to improve the pace of key processes.

Innovation and new learning will characterize the successful organization in the 21st century. OC consultants must help client organizations to develop these characteristics. All successful organizations in the 21st century will be "learning organizations" (Beitler, 2010).

Organizational change consultants have always had an interdisciplinary approach to practice (e.g., adult psychology, group dynamics, organizational theory). This interdisciplinary approach will have to expand further in the future. OC consultants will also have to draw from management theory, cultural analysis, political theory, cognitive science, social psychology, and other social sciences.

More diverse client organizations, with organizational structures beyond anything we can comprehend today, will require OC consultants who possess extensive knowledge of business theory and practice.

Obviously, OC practice must become more cross cultural as business becomes more global. Cummings and Worley (2008, p.622) states, "Despite increased research and practice in this area, we know little about planned change processes in cross-cultural settings." I hope to see more OC consultants who work with international clients publishing their experiences in the form of case studies. I believe OC consulting opportunities will be extremely plentiful and challenging in the coming years, especially in Eastern Europe, Asia, and Africa.

Lastly, I agree with Cummings and Worley (2008) that OC values will evolve and become clearer in the 21st century. OC theory and practice must maintain a dual focus on individual development (a humanistic approach) and organizational development (an efficiency approach). I believe the two are highly compatible.

As I said at the beginning of this book, I believe OC is an exciting and rewarding profession. I believe the opportunities in the 21st century are limitless. I hope you will join me in this exciting and rewarding work!

REFERENCES

Beitler, M.A. (1999). Learning and development agreements for mid-career professionals. *Performance in Practice*, Fall 1999, American Society for Training and Development.

Beitler, M.A. (2000). Contract learning in organizational learning and management development. In H.B. Long and Associates (Eds.), *Practice and theory in self-directed learning*. Schaumberg, IL: Motorola University Press.

Beitler, M.A. (2010). *Strategic organizational learning* (2nd ed.). Greensboro, NC: Practitioner Press International.

Cummings, T.G. & Worley, C.G. (2008). *Organization development and change* (9th ed.). Cincinnati, OH: South-Western.

Dunning, J.H. (1999). The changing nature of firms and governments in a knowledge-based globalized economy. In J. Engelhard & W.A. Oechsler (Eds.), *Internationales management*. Wiesbaden, Germany: Gabler.

Hofstede, G. (2001). *Culture's consequences* (2nd ed.). Beverly Hills, CA: Sage Publications.

Hofstede, G. (1993). Cultural constraints in management theories. *Academy of Management Executive*, 7(1), 81-94.

Kurzweil, R. (2006) *The singularity is near: When humans transcend biology*. New York: Penguin Books.

Mendenhall, M. & Oddou, G. (1985). The dimensions of expatriate acculturation: A review. *Academy of Management Review*, 10(1), 39-47.

Oechsler, W.A. (1999). Global management and local systems of employment relations. In J. Engelhard & W. A. Oechsler (Eds.), *Internationales Management*. Wiesbaden, Germany: Gabler.

Oechsler, W.A. (2000). Workplace and workforce 2000+: The future of our work environment. *International Archives of Occupational Environmental Health*, Vol.73 supplement (June).

Orlikowski, W.J. (1988). The data processing occupation: Professionalization or proletarianization? *Research in the Sociology of Work*, 4, 95-124.

Schein, E. (2010). *Organizational culture and leadership* (4th ed). San Francisco: Jossey-Bass.

Stewart, T.A. (1997). *Intellectual capital*. London: Oxford.

Trompenaars, F. (2011). *Riding the waves of culture: Understanding diversity in global business* (3rd ed.). New York: McGraw-Hill.

Van Maanen, J. & Barley, S.R. (1984). Occupational communities: Culture and control in organizations. In B.M. Staw & L.L. Cummings (Eds.), *Research in organizational behavior* (Vol. 6). Greenwich, Conn: JAI Press.

Zuboff, S. (1988). *In the age of the smart machine*. New York: Basic Books.

Appendices
Comprehensive Reference List

Ackerman, M.S. (2000). The intellectual challenge of CSCW: The gap between social requirements and technical feasibility. *Human-Computer Interaction*, 15, 179-203.

Abrahamson, E. (1996). Management fashion. *Academy of Management Review*, 21, pp.254-285.

Adler, A. (1929). *The science of living*. New York: Greenberg.

Argyris, C. & Schön, D. (1976). *Organizational learning*. Reading, MA: Addison-Wesley.

Ashkenas, R., DeMonaco, L., & Francis, S. (1998). Making the deal real: How GE Capital integrates acquisitions. *Harvard Business Review* (January-February).

Bandura, A. (1977). *Social learning theory*. Englewood Cliffs, NJ: Prentice-Hall.

Baskett, M. (1993). *Workplace factors that enhance self-directed learning*. (Text No. 93-01-002). Montreal, Canada: Group for Interdisciplinary research on Autonomy and Training, University of Quebec at Montreal.

Beckhard, R. (1967). The confrontation meeting. *Harvard Business Review*, 45 (March-April), pp.149-155.

Beckhard, R. & Harris, R. (1987). *Organizational transitions: Managing complex change* (2nd ed.). Reading, MA: Addison- Wesley.

Beer, M. (1980). *Organizational change and development: A systems view*. Santa Monica, CA: Goodyear Publishing.

Beitler, M.A. (1999). Learning and development agreements with mid-career professionals. *Performance in Practice*, Fall 1999. American Society for Training & Development.

Beitler, M.A. (2000). Contract learning in organizational learning and management development. In H.B. Long and Associates (Eds.), *Practice and theory in self-directed learning*. Schaumberg, IL: Motorola University Press.

Beitler, M.A. (2001). Self-directed learning readiness at General Motors Japan. In H.B. Long and Associates (Eds.), *Expanding horizons in self-directed learning*. Schaumberg, IL: Motorola University Press.

Beitler, M.A. (2010). *Strategic organizational learning (2nd ed.)*. Greensboro, NC: Practitioner Press International.

Blake, R., Shepard, H., & Mouton, J. (1965). *Managing intergroup conflict in industry*. Houston, TX: Gulf Publishing.

Bowers, D. (1973). OD techniques and their results in 23 organizations: The Michigan ICL study. *Journal of Applied Behavioral Science* (January-March), pp.21-43.

Brockett, R. & Hiemstra, R. (1991). *Self-direction in adult learning: Perspectives on theory, research, and practice*. London: Routledge.

Buller, P.F. (1988). For successful strategic change: Blend OD practices with strategic management. *Organizational Dynamics*, 16, pp.42-55.

Buono, A. (2000). Personal correspondence

Burke, W.W. (1982). *Organization development: Principles and practices*. Boston: Little, Brown, & Co.

Cameron, K.S., Freeman, S.J., & Mishra, A.K. (1991). Best practices in white-collar downsizing: Managing contradictions. *Academy of Management Executive*, 5, 57-73.

Cameron, K.S. & Quinn, R.E. (1999). *Diagnosing and changing organizational culture*. Reading, MA: Addison-Wesley.

Chisolm, R. (1998). *Developing network organizations: Learning from theory and practice*. Reading, MA: Addison-Wesley.

Chuprina, L. & Durr, R. (2001). Implications of foreign culture and SDL on expatriate managers at Motorola, Inc. In H.B. Long & Associates (Eds.), *Self-directed learning in the new millennium*. Schaumberg, IL: Motorola University Press.

Clark, T. (1995). *Managing consultants: Consultancy as the management of impressions*. Buckingham, England: Open University Press.

Confessore, S.J. & Kops, W.J. (1998). Self-directed learning and the learning organization: Examining the connection between the individual and the learning environment. *Human Resource Development Quarterly*, 9(4), pp.365-375.

Cooperrider, D. & Srivastva, S. (1987). Appreciative inquiry in organizational life. In R. Woodman & W. Pasmore (Eds.), *Research in organizational change and development*, Vol. 1. Greenwich, CT: JAI Press. (pp.129-169)

Cummings, T.G. & Worley, C.G. (2008). *Organization development and change* (9th ed.). Cincinnati, OH: South-Western.

Delahaye, B.L. & Smith, H.E. (1995). The validity of the Learning Preference Assessment. *Adult Education Quarterly*, 45(3), pp.159-173.

Denison, D.R. (1990). *Corporate culture and organizational effectiveness*. New York: John Wiley.

Dixon, N.M. (1994). Organizational learning: A review of the literature with implications for HRD professionals. *Human Resource Development Quarterly*, 3(1), pp.29-49.

Dunning, J.H. (1999). The changing nature of firms and governments in a knowledge-based globalized economy. In J. Engelhard & W.A. Oechsler (Eds.), *Internationales management*. Wiesbaden, Germany: Gabler.

Eisenhardt, K. (1989). Agency theory: An assessment and review. *Academy of Management Review*, 14, pp.57-77.

Ellis, A. & Dryden, W. (1987). *The practice of rational-emotive therapy*. New York: Springer Publishing.

Emerson, R.M. (1962). Power-dependence relations. *American Sociological Review*, 27, pp.31-40.

Emery, M. & Purser, R.E. (1996). *The search conference*. San Francisco: Jossey-Bass.

Ernst, B. & Kieser, A. (2002) In search of explanations for the consulting explosion. In L. Engwall & K. Sahlin-Andersson (Eds.), *The expansion of management knowledge: carriers, ideas, and circulation*. Stanford, CA: Stanford University Press.

Fisher, R., Ury, W., & Patton, B. (1991). *Getting to yes* (2nd ed.). New York: Penguin Books.

Fordyce, J.K. & Weil, R. (1971). *Managing with people*. Reading, MA: Addison-Wesley.

Foucher, R. (1995). *Enhancing self-directed learning in the workplace: A model and a research agenda*. (Text No. 95-01- 005). Montreal, Canada: Group for Interdisciplinary Research on Autonomy and Training, University of Quebec at Montreal.

French, J.R.P. & Raven, B. (1959). The bases of social power. In D. Cartwright (Ed.), *Studies in social power*. Ann Arbor, MI: Institute for Social Research, University of Michigan. (pp.150-167).

French, W.L. & Bell, C.H., Jr. (1999). *Organization development: Behavioral science interventions for organization Improvement* (6th ed.). Upper Saddle River, NJ: Prentice-Hall.

Friedlander, F. & Brown, L. (1974). Organization development. In M. Rosenzweig & L. Porter (Eds.), *Annual Review of Psychology*. Palo Alto, CA: Annual Review.

Furusten, S. (1998). The creation of popular management texts. In J.L. Alvarez (Ed.), *The diffusion and consumption of business knowledge* (pp.141-163). London: McMillan.

Galbraith, J. & Lawler, E. (1993). *Organizing for the future: The new logic for managing complex organizations*. San Francisco: Jossey-Bass.

Galpin, T. & Robinson, D. (1997). Merger integration: The ultimate change management challenge. *Mergers and Acquisitions*, 31, pp.24-29.

Garrison, D.R. (1987). Self-directed and distance learning: Facilitating self-directed learning beyond the institutional setting. *International Journal of Lifelong Education*, 6(4), pp.309-318.

Goldman, D. (2000). Leadership that gets results. *Harvard Business Review*, March-April.

Goodman, P. & Dean, J. (1982). Creating long-term organizational Change. In P. Goodman (Ed.), *Change in organization*, (pp.226-79). San Francisco: Jossey-Bass.

Greiner, L.E. & Schein, V.E. (1988). *Power and organization development: Mobilizing power to implement change*. Reading, MA: Addison-Wesley.

Guglielmino, L.M. (1997). Reliability and validity of the Self- Directed Learning Readiness Scale and the Learning Preference Assessment. In H.B. Long & Associates, *Expanding horizons in self-directed learning* (pp.209-222). Norman, OK: College of Education, University of Oklahoma.

Guglielmino, L.M. (1978). Development of the Self-Directed Learning Readiness Scale (Doctoral dissertation, University of Georgia, 1977). *Dissertation Abstracts International*, 1978, 38, 6467A.

Guglielmino, L.M. & Guglielmino, P.J. (1991a). *Expanding your readiness for self-directed learning: A workbook for the Learning Preference Assessment.* King of Prussia, PA: Organization Design and Development.

Guglielmino, L.M. & Guglielmino, P.J. (1991b). *Learning Preference Assessment facilitator guide.* King of Prussia, PA: Organization Design and Development.

Hackman, J.R. & Morris, C. (1975). Group tasks, group interaction process, and group performance effectiveness: A review and proposed integration. In L. Berkowitz (Ed.), *Advances in Experimental Social Psychology*, Vol. 9. New York: Academic Press.

Hackman, J.R. & Oldham, G.R. (1975). Development of the Job Diagnostic Survey. *Journal of Applied Psychology*, 60, 159- 170.

Hackman, J.R. & Oldham, G.R. (1976). Motivation through the design of work: Test of a theory. *Organizational Behavior and Human Performance*, 16, 250-279.

Hackman, J.R. & Oldham, G.R. (1980). *Work redesign*. Reading, MA: Addison-Wesley.

Hanna, D.P. (1988). *Designing organizations for high performance*. Reading, MA: Addison-Wesley.

Hansen, M., Nohria, N., & Tierney, T. (2001). What's your strategy for managing knowledge? Chapter in *Harvard Business Review on Organizational*. Boston, MA: Harvard Business School Publishing.

Hofstede, G. (2001). *Culture's consequences (2nd ed.)*. Beverly Hills, CA: Sage Publications.

Hofstede, G. (1993). Cultural constraints in management theories. *Academy of Management Executive*, 7(1), 81-94.

Jacobs, R.W. (1994). *Real time strategic change*. San Francisco: Berrett-Koehler.

Kieser, A. (1997). Myth and rhetoric in management fashion. *Organization*, 4 (1), 49-74.

Kieser, A. (2002). On communication barriers between management science, consultancies, and business organizations. In T. Clark & R. Fincham (Eds.), *Critical consulting: New perspectives on the management advice industry*. Oxford, UK: Blackwell Publishers.

Knowles, M. (1975). *Self-directed learning: A guide for learners and teachers*. Chicago: Follett.

Knowles, M. (1986). Using contract learning. San Francisco: Jossey-Bass.

Kotter, J.P. (1996). *Leading change.* Boston, MA: Harvard Business School Press.

Kotter, J.P. & Heskett, J.L. (1992). *Corporate culture and performance.* New York: Free Press.

Krough, von G. & Roos, J. (1995). *Organizational epistemology.* London: Mcmillan.

Kurzweil, R. (2006). *The singularity is near: When humans transcend biology.* New York: Penguin Books.

Lewin, A.Y. & Minton, J.W. (1986). Determining organizational Effectiveness: Another look, and an agenda for research. *Management Science,* 32, pp.514-538.

Lippitt, G. (1970). Developing life plans. *Training and Development Journal,* May, pp.2-7.

Long, H.B. (1989). Truth unguessed and yet to be discovered: A professional's self-directed learning. In H.B. Long & Associates, *Self-directed learning: Emerging theory and practice* (pp.125-135). Norman, OK: Oklahoma Research Center for Continuing, Professional, and Higher Education of the University of Oklahoma.

Long, H.B. (1990). Psychological control in self-directed learning. *International Journal of Lifelong Education,* 9(4), 331-38.

Long, H.B. (1991). Challenges in the study and practice of self- directed learning. In H. B. Long & Associates, *Self-directed learning: Consensus and conflict* (pp.11-28). Norman, OK: Oklahoma Research Center for Continuing, Professional, and Higher Education of the University of Oklahoma.

Long, H.B. & Ageykum, S. (1988). Self-directed learning: Assessment and validation. In H.B. Long & Associates, *Self- directed learning: Application and theory* (pp.253-266). Athens, GA: Adult Education Department, University of Georgia.

Long, H.B. & Morris, S.(1995). Self-directed learning in business and industry: A review of the literature 1983-1993. In H.B. Long & Associates (Eds.), *New dimensions in self-directed learning.* Norman, OK: College of Education, University of Oklahoma.

March, J.G. (1991). Organizational consultants and organizational research. *Journal of Applied Communication Research,* 19, 20-31.

March, J.G. & Sutton, R.I. (1997). Organizational performance as a dependent variable. *Organization Science,* 8 (6), pp.698 -706.

Marshak, R.J. (1993). Managing the metaphors of change. *Organizational Dynamics,* Summer.

McCaskey, M. (1997). Framework for analyzing work groups. *Harvard Business School Case 9-480-009.* Boston: Harvard Business School.

McCune, S.K. (1989). A meta-analytic study of adult self- direction in learning: A review of the research from 1977 to 1987 (Doctoral dissertation, Texas A&M University, 1988). *Dissertation Abstracts International*, 1989, 49, 3237.

McCune, S.K., Guglielmino, L.M., & Garcia, G. (1990). Adult self-direction in learning: A preliminary meta-analytic investigation of research using the Self-Directed Learning Readiness Scale. In H.B. Long & Associates, *Advances in self-directed learning research* (pp.145-156). Norman, OK: Oklahoma Research Center for Continuing, Professional, and Higher Education of the University of Oklahoma.

Meister, J. (1998). *Corporate universities*, (rev. ed.). New York: McGraw-Hill.

Melamed, S., Ben-Avi, I., Luz, J., & Green, M. (1995). Objective and subjective work monitoring: Effects on job satisfaction, psychological distress, and absenteeism in blue-collar workers. *Journal of Applied Psychology*, 80, 29-42.

Mendenhall, M. & Oddou, G. (1985). The dimensions of expatriate acculturation: A review. *Academy of Management Review*, 10(1), 39-47.

Merriam, S. & Brockett, R. (1997). *The profession and practice of adult education*. San Francisco: Jossey-Bass.

Mintzberg, H. (1983). *Power in and around organizations*. Englewood Cliffs, NJ: Prentice-Hall. (pp.24-26).

Muchinsky, P.M. (2000). *Psychology applied to work* (6th ed.). Belmont, CA: Wadsworth/ Thomson Learning.

Oechsler, W.A. (1999). Global management and local systems of employment relations. In J. Engelhard & W. A. Oechsler (Eds.), *Internationales Management*. Wiesbaden, Germany: Gabler.

Oechsler, W.A. (2000). Workplace and workforce 2000+: The future of our work environment. *International Archives of Occupational Environmental Health*, Vol.73 supplement (June).

Orlikowski, W.J. (1988). The data processing occupation: Professionalization or proletarianization? *Research in the Sociology of Work*, 4, 95-124.

Nohria, N. & Eccles, R. (1998). Where does management knowledge come from? In J.L. Alvarez (Ed.), *The diffusion and consumption of business knowledge*, pp.278-304. London: McMillan.

Pasmore, W. (1976). Backfeed, the Michigan ICL study revisited: An alternative explanation of the results. *Journal of Applied Behavioral Science* (April-June), pp. 245-51.

Porter, M. (1980). *Competitive strategy*. New York: Free Press.

Porter, M. (1985). *Competitive advantage*. New York: Free Press.

Robinson, S.L., Kraatz, M.S., & Rousseau, D.M. (1994). Changing obligations and the psychological contract: A longitudinal study. *Academy of Management Journal*, 37, 137-152.

Rogers, T.H. (1981). *Strategic planning: A major OD intervention.* ASTD Publications.

Salancik, G. & Pfeffer, J. (1977). Who gets power — and how they hold on to it: A strategic-contingency model of power. *Organizational Dynamics,* 5, p.3.

Schein, E.H. (1978). *Career dynamics: Matching individual and organizational needs.* Reading, MA: Addison-Wesley.

Schein, E.H. (1983). The role of the founder in creating organizational culture. *Organizational Dynamics,* Summer, pp.13-28.

Schein, E.H. (1987). *The clinical perspective in fieldwork.* Newbury Park, CA: Sage.

Schein, E.H. (1987). Individuals and careers. In J.W. Lorsch (Ed.), *Handbook of organizational behavior.* Englewood Cliffs, NJ: Prentice-Hall.

Schein, E.H. (1999). *Process consultation revisited: Building the helping relationship.* Reading, MA: Addison-Wesley.

Schein, E.H. (2010). *Organizational culture and leadership* (4th ed). San Francisco: Jossey-Bass.

Schreyögg, G., Oechsler, W., & Wächter, H. (1995). *Managing in a European context.* Wiesbaden, Germany: Gabler.

Senge, P.M. (1990). *The fifth discipline: The art and practice of the learning organization.* New York: Doubleday.

Stewart, T.A. (1997). *Intellectual capital.* London: Oxford.

Summer, C.E. (1980). *Strategic behavior in business and government.* Boston: Little, Brown.

Taylor, F.W. (1911). *The principles of scientific management.* New York: Harper & Row.

Thompson, S.C. (1981). Will it hurt less if I can control it? A complex answer to a simple question. *Psychological Bulletin,* 90, 89-101.

Tough, A. (1979). *The adult's learning projects* (2nd ed.). Toronto: Ontario Institute for Studies in Education.

Trice, H. & Beyer, J. (1993). *The cultures of work organizations.* Englewood Cliffs, NJ: Prentice-Hall.

Trist, E., Higgin, B., Murray, H., & Pollock, A. (1963). *Organizational choice.* London: Tavistock.

Trompenaars, F. (2011). *Riding the waves of culture: Understanding diversity in global business (3rd ed.).* New York: McGraw-Hill.

Turner, A.N. & Lawrence, P.R. (1965). *Industrial jobs and the worker: An investigation of response to task attributes.* Cambridge, MA: Harvard University Press.

Ulrich, D. (1999). *Results-based leadership.* Boston, MA: Harvard Business School Press.

Van Maanen, J. & Barley, S.R. (1984). Occupational communities: Culture and control in organizations. In B.M. Staw & L.L. Cummings (Eds.), *Research in organizational behavior* (Vol. 6). Greenwich, Conn: JAI Press.

Weber, W. (1990). *Basic content analysis*. Thousand Oaks, CA: Sage Publishing.

Weisbord, M.R. (1987). *Productive workplaces*. San Francisco: Jossey-Bass.

Wong, C. & Campion, M.A. (1991). Development and test of a task level model of motivational job design. *Journal of Applied Psychology*, 76, 825-837.

Worley, C., Hitchin, D., & Ross, W. (1996). *Integrated strategic change: How OD helps build competitive advantage*. Reading, MA: Addison-Wesley.

Zuboff, S. (1988). *In the age of the smart machine*. New York: Basic Books.

Subject Index

Name Index

About the Author

Dr. Michael Beitler (pronounced Bite-ler) began his 35-year career as a management consultant with one of the world's largest consulting firms. He has earned an international reputation as a keynote speaker, workshop leader, consultant, and executive coach.

Mike's clients include Fortune 500 companies and mid-sized companies in manufacturing, distribution, retailing, banking, publishing, and professional services, as well Federal and State government.

Dr. Beitler's teaching experience includes the MBA programs of the University of North Carolina at Greensboro and the University of Mannheim's Business School (Germany's #1 ranked business school).

Mike's books and articles are used at leading universities in the U.S., Canada, Europe, and Asia (including Cornell University and NYU), and at leading corporations (including Coca-Cola and Wells Fargo).

Please contact Mike about speaking and consulting, or with your comments and suggestions about this book, at:

Internet: www.mikebeitler.com
E-mail: mike@mikebeitler.com
Mail: P.O. Box 38353
Greensboro, NC 27438 USA